Managerial Paper P2
Management Accounting – Decision Management

First edition January 2005

ISBN 0 7517 1962 5

British Library Cataloguing-in-Publication Data

A catalogue record for this book is available from the British Library

Published by
BPP Professional Education, Aldine House, Aldine Place, London W12 8AW
www.bpp.com

Printed in Great Britain by Ashford Colour Press

Welcome to BPP's CIMA **Passcards** for Paper P2 *Management Accounting – Decision Management*.

- They **save you time**. Important topics are summarised for you.

- They incorporate **diagrams** to kick start your memory.

- They follow the overall **structure** of the BPP Study Texts, but BPP's CIMA **Passcards** are not just a condensed book. Each card has been separately designed for clear presentation. Topics are self contained and can be grasped visually.

- CIMA **Passcards** are **just the right size** for pockets, briefcases and bags.

- CIMA **Passcards focus on the exam** you will be facing.

Run through the complete set of **Passcards** as often as you can during your final revision period. The day before the exam, try to go through the **Passcards** again! You will then be well on your way to passing your exams.

Good luck!

Topic List

Relevant costs

Assumptions and non-quantifiable factors

It is important to realise that decision-making questions are likely to ask you to discuss non-quantifiable factors as well as require you to carry out calculations to support a particular decision option. So don't neglect these non-quantifiable issues. And, as always, remember to state any assumptions you make.

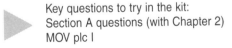

Key questions to try in the kit:
Section A questions (with Chapter 2)
MOV plc I

Relevant costs are ──┐ future
                     ├── incremental
                     └── cash flows

The relevance of fixed costs

Unless given an indication to the contrary, assume fixed costs are irrelevant and variable costs are relevant.

Examples

Avoidable costs are costs which would not be incurred if the activity to which they relate did not exist.

A **differential cost** is the difference in total costs between alternatives.

An **opportunity cost** is the benefit which would have been earned, but which has been given up, by choosing one option instead of another.

- **Directly attributable fixed costs**, although fixed within a relevant range or regarded as fixed because management has set a budgeted expenditure level, are relevant because they do one of two things.
  - □ Increase if certain activities are undertaken
  - □ Decrease/are eliminated if a decision is taken to reduce the scale of operations/shutdown entirely
- **General fixed overheads** (such as an apportioned share of head office charges) are unaffected by a change in the scale of operations and are irrelevant.

Non-relevant costs

Cost	Description	Example
Sunk costs	Expenditure which has already been incurred and charged, or which has already been incurred or which relates to an expenditure decision which has irrevocably been taken, and which will be charged in a future accounting period	Development costs already incurred
Committed costs	Future cash outflows that will be incurred regardless of the decision taken	Contracts already entered into
Notional costs	Hypothetical accounting costs which reflect the use of a benefit for which no actual cash expense is incurred	Notional rent
Historical costs		

1: Relevant cash flows for decisions

Identifying relevant costs

Example

Machinery user costs

- Once a machine has been bought its cost is a sunk cost.
- Depreciation is not a relevant cost because it is not a cash flow.
- Using machinery may involve some relevant incremental user costs (hire charges, fall in resale value of owned assets).

Example

Materials

- The relevant cost is generally current replacement cost.
- If materials have been purchased but will not be replaced, the relevant cost is the higher of the following.
  - Current resale value
  - Value if put to an alternative use
- If there is no resale value and no other use, the relevant cost is nil.

Example

Labour

- Costs are often not incremental because the labour force will be paid irrespective of the decision made.
- If the labour force can be put to an alternative use, the relevant cost is the sum of the following.
  - The variable costs of the labour and associated variable overheads
  - The contribution forgone from not being able to put the workforce to its alternative use

| Relevant cost of a scarce resource | = | contribution / incremental profit forgone from the next best opportunity for using the scarce resource (**opportunity cost**) | + | variable cost of the scarce resource (cash expenditure to purchase it, if it has not already been purchased) |

Example

| Relevant cost per hour of scarce machine time | = | contribution per hour from hiring out a machine as opposed to using it | + | running cost per hour of the machine |

Remember that, for short-term decisions, costs need to be divided into those that vary in the short term with the volume of activity (**short-term variable costs**) and those that remain constant over wide ranges of activity for a specified time period (**fixed costs**).

Assumptions in relevant costing

- Cost behaviour patterns are known.

- The amount of fixed costs, unit variable costs, sales price and sales demand are known with certainty.

- The objective of decision making in the short term is to maximise 'satisfaction', which is often regarded as 'short-term profit'.

- The information on which a decision is based is complete and reliable.

For once-only decisions, or decisions affecting the use of marginal spare capacity, absorption costing information about unit profits is irrelevant and misleading.

Non-quantifiable factors in decision making

- The availability of cash
- Employees
- Customers
- Competitors
- Timing factors
- Suppliers
- Feasibility
- Flexibility and internal control
- Unquantified opportunity costs
- Political pressures
- Legal constraints
- Inflation

2: Short-term decisions

Decision-making questions will build on the knowledge you gained in your earlier studies and, as well as requiring you to perform calculations, will ask you to consider non-quantifiable issues.

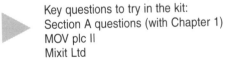

Key questions to try in the kit:
Section A questions (with Chapter 1)
MOV plc II
Mixit Ltd

Acceptance/rejection of contracts

If an organisation does not have spare capacity, existing business should only be turned away if the contribution from a contract is greater than the contribution from the business which must be sacrificed.

Minimum pricing

The minimum price for a one-off product or service contract is its total relevant cost. This is the price at which the company would make no incremental profit or loss from undertaking the work, but would just achieve an incremental cost breakeven point.

Extra shift decisions and overtime

The decision to work an extra shift should be taken on the basis of whether the costs of the shift are exceeded by the benefits to be obtained.

The key point in decision-making questions is to let the marker see what you are doing.

- Number your workings consecutively.
- Label tables and workings with headings and show units (£, kgs, etc).
- On a separate page, do a summary and state your conclusion.
- Cross reference your summary to your workings.

No scarce resources

The relevant costs of the decision are the differential costs between making and buying.

> **Further considerations**
>
> - How to use freed up capacity
> - Could using an outside supplier cause an industrial dispute?
> - Subcontractor delivery reliability and product quality
> - Loss of flexibility and control by subcontracting

With scarce resources

If an organisation has to subcontract because of insufficient in-house resources, total costs are minimised if those units bought have the lowest extra variable cost of buying (compared with making in-house) per unit of scarce resource saved by buying.

Example (limited labour time)

	A	B
Variable cost of making	£16	£14
Variable cost of buying	£20	£19
Extra variable cost of buying	£4	£5
Labour hours saved by buying	2	2
Extra variable cost of buying per hour saved	£2	£2.50
Priority for making in-house	2nd	1st

The best approach is to draw up a three-column table with columns for the first option, for the second option and for the differences between the options.

- Do savings and costs separately and put one type in brackets. It doesn't matter which way round you do this as long as you are consistent within the question.
- Subtract column 2 from column 1, taking care with minus signs: −50,000 −(−45,000) = −5,000

Example

		Option 1 £	Option 2 £	Net (savings)/ costs £
Savings	Saving 1	(500)	(100)	(400)
	Saving 2	(300)	(600)	300
Costs	Cost 1	0	200	(200)
	Cost 2	700	0	700
Net cost				400

Conclusion. Option 1 costs £400 more than option 2. (Alternatively, option 2 would bring savings of £400 more than option 1.)

Shutdown problems involve decisions about whether to close down a product line, department or other activity, perhaps because it is making losses or running costs are too expensive and if the decision is to shut down, whether the closure should be permanent or temporary.

Other (non-quantifiable) considerations

In practice this sort of decision has long-term consequences.

- Is the closure to be a permanent reduction in capacity, and is this desirable?
- What is the impact on employees, customers, competitors and suppliers?

Financial considerations

The basic method is to use short-run relevant costs to calculate contributions and profits or losses.

1   Calculate what is earned by the process at present (perhaps in comparison with others).

2   Calculate what will be the financial consequences of closing down (selling machines, redundancy costs etc).

3   Compare the results and act accordingly.

4   Bear in mind that some fixed costs may no longer be incurred if the decision is to shut down and they are therefore relevant to the decision.

2: Short-term decisions

Joint products

Two or more products produced by the same process and separated in processing, each having a sufficiently high saleable value to merit recognition as a main product

Distinguishing features of joint products

- They are produced in the same process.
- They are indistinguishable from each other until the separation point.
- They each have a substantial sales value (after further processing, if necessary).
- They may require future processing after the separation point.

Apportioning joint costs

Costs incurred up to the point of separation (**split-off point**) need to be apportioned between the joint products for the purposes of stock valuation, profitability analysis and pricing.

> **Joint product costs are not used for decision making.**

There are four methods of doing this.

1: Physical measurement

- Cost is apportioned on the basis of the proportion that the output of each product bears by weight or volume to the total output.

- It is unsuitable where products separate during processing into different states.

- It ignores sales value and may lead to inappropriate results if sales values and volumes differ significantly.

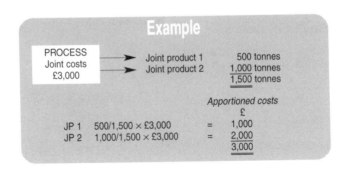

Example			
PROCESS Joint costs £3,000	→ Joint product 1 → Joint product 2		500 tonnes 1,000 tonnes 1,500 tonnes
			Apportioned costs £
JP 1	500/1,500 × £3,000	=	1,000
JP 2	1,000/1,500 × £3,000	=	2,000 3,000

2: Short-term decisions

2: Sales value at split-off point

Cost is apportioned according to products' ability to produce income (that is, in the proportions that the sales value of the products bear to the sales value of the process's total output).

3: Sales value minus further processing costs

If the sales value at split-off point is not available, costs can be apportioned on the basis of residual / notional / proxy sales value (final sales value minus further processing costs).

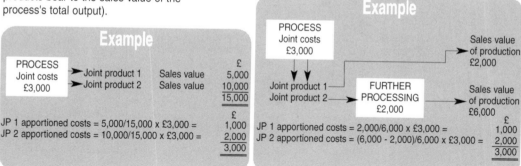

Example

```
                                                    £
PROCESS      → Joint product 1   Sales value      5,000
Joint costs  → Joint product 2   Sales value     10,000
£3,000                                            15,000
```

```
                                                    £
JP 1 apportioned costs = 5,000/15,000 x £3,000 =   1,000
JP 2 apportioned costs = 10,000/15,000 x £3,000 =  2,000
                                                   3,000
```

Example

```
PROCESS                                    Sales value
Joint costs                              → of production
£3,000                                      £2,000

Joint product 1 ——      FURTHER
Joint product 2 ——     PROCESSING          Sales value
                        £2,000            → of production
                                            £6,000
```

```
                                                         £
JP 1 apportioned costs = 2,000/6,000 x £3,000 =         1,000
JP 2 apportioned costs = (6,000 - 2,000)/6,000 x £3,000 = 2,000
                                                         3,000
```

4: Weighted average method

If 'units' of joint product are not comparable in terms of physical resemblance or physical weight (gas, liquid, solid etc), joint costs are apportioned on the basis of 'weighted units' (units of joint product × weighting factor).

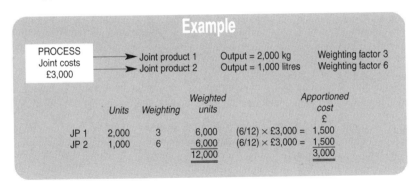

Example

PROCESS
Joint costs
£3,000

→ Joint product 1   Output = 2,000 kg   Weighting factor 3
→ Joint product 2   Output = 1,000 litres   Weighting factor 6

	Units	Weighting	Weighted units		Apportioned cost £
JP 1	2,000	3	6,000	(6/12) × £3,000 =	1,500
JP 2	1,000	6	6,000	(6/12) × £3,000 =	1,500
			12,000		3,000

Further processing decision

A product should be further processed if its sales revenue minus its further processing costs exceeds its sales revenue at the split-off point. The apportionment of joint processing costs is irrelevant to the decision.

By-products

A supplementary or secondary product (arising as the result of a process), the value of which is small relative to that of the principal product(s)

Possible accounting treatments of by-products

Do NOT allocate joint costs to a by-product.

- Add the net sales revenue from the by-product to sales revenue of the main product.
- Treat the sales revenue of the by-product as a separate incidental source of revenue ('other income').
- Deduct the sales revenue of the by-product from the cost of production/sales of the main product.
- Deduct the net realisable value of the by-product from the cost of production of the main product (most common method).

The choice of method will be influenced by the circumstances of production and ease of calculation, as much as by conceptual correctness. The method you are most likely to come across in examinations is the last method.

Topic List

Demand

Other issues in pricing decisions

Profit maximisation

Cost-based approaches

Strategies

Historically, price setting was the single most important decision made by the sales department and the typical reaction was to cut prices in order to sell more. Modern businesses, however, seek to interpret and satisfy customer wants and needs by modifying existing products or introducing new ones.

Not withstanding this 'change' in emphasis, pricing is still very important, in terms of profitability, survival and as a competitive tool.

Key questions to try in the kit:
Section A questions
Off-the-shelf I and II
Mobile telephones

Price elasticity of demand (η)

A measure of the extent of change in market demand for a good, in response to a change in its price

= change in quantity demanded, as a % of demand ÷ change in price, as a % of price

Inelastic demand

- $\eta < 1$
- Steep demand curve
- Demand falls by a smaller % than % rise in price
- Pricing decision: increase prices

Elastic demand

- $\eta > 1$
- Shallow demand curve
- Demand falls by a larger % than % rise in price
- Pricing decision: decide whether change in cost will be less than change in revenue

Factors determining the degree of elasticity

- The price of the good
- The price of other goods
- The size and distribution of household incomes
- Tastes and fashion
- Expectations
- Obsolescence

Degrees of elasticity

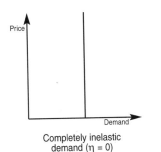

Completely inelastic
demand ($\eta = 0$)

Demand is totally
unresponsive to
changes in price.

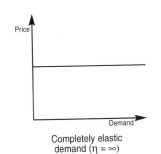

Completely elastic
demand ($\eta = \infty$)

Demand is limitless at
price P but non-
existent above price P.

Elastic demand

The 'normal' situation,
demand increasing as
prices are lowered.

Demand and the individual firm

The volume of demand for one organisation's goods rather than another's is influenced by three principal factors.

1 **Product life cycle (PLC)**

- Introduction — potential customers unaware of product, advertising needed
- Growth — demand increases
- Maturity — modifications/improvements to sustain demand
- Decline — market will have bought enough of the product

2 **Quality** — the better the quality, the greater the demand

3 **Marketing (4 Ps)**

- Price
- Product
- Place — potential buyers will turn to substitutes if a good is difficult to obtain
- Promotion — brand names, shop displays and free gifts will stimulate demand

Markets

The price that an organisation can charge will be determined to some degree by the market in which it operates.

- Perfect competition
- Monopolistic competition
- Monopoly
- Oligopoly

Competition

How to fight a price war

- Sell on value, not on price
- Target service
- Use 'package pricing'
- Make price comparisons difficult
- Build up key accounts
- Explore new pricing models

Other factors which influence price

- Price sensitivity of purchasers (eg business traveller considers level of service rather than price)
- Price perception (eg designer labels)
- Compatibility with other products
- Competitors' actions and reactions
- Suppliers' prices
- Inflation
- Quality connotations
- Income effects (eg during a recession)
- Substitute products
- Ethics

Deriving the demand curve

If demand is linear the equation for the demand curve is

$$P = a - \frac{bQ}{\Delta Q}$$

where P = price

Q = quantity demanded

a = price at which demand would be nil

b = amount by which price rises for each stepped change in demand

ΔQ = stepped change (decrease) in demand

Example

P = £10
Q = 100 units
Q falls to 95 units if P rises to £11.

a = £10 + ((100/5) × 1) = £30

P = 30 − Q/5

$$a = \pounds(\text{current price}) + \left(\frac{\text{current quantity at current price}}{\text{change in quantity when price changed by £b}} \times \pounds b \right)$$

Example: without using the demand curve formula

Maximum demand for LM Ltd's product is 7,000 units per annum.
Demand will reduce by 150 units for every £1 increase in the selling price.

∴ When p = 0, demand (x) = 7,000
  When p = 1, demand (x) = 6,850

∴ Demand (x) = 7,000 − 150p, where p is the selling price in £
  (because demand will drop by 150 units for every increase (from £0) of £1 in the selling price)

If the profit-maximising annual sales level is, say, 4,000 units, the profit-maximising selling price can be calculated.

  x = 7,000 − 150p
  If x = 4,000, p = £20

Determining the profit-maximising selling price/output level

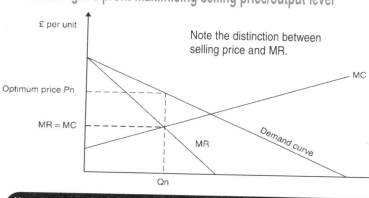

Note the distinction between selling price and MR.

Method 1: using equations

Profits are maximised when MC = MR.

Example

$MC = 320 - 0.2x$

$MR = 1,920 - 16.2x$

∴ Profits are maximised when
$320 - 0.2x = 1,920 - 16.2x$
ie when $x = 100$

You could also be provided with/asked to determine the demand curve in order to calculate the price at this profit-maximising output level.

Method 2: visual inspection of tabulation of data

1 Work out the demand curve and hence the price and total revenue (PQ) at various levels of demand.

2 Calculate total cost and hence marginal cost at each level of demand.

3 Calculate profit at each level of demand, thereby determining the price and level of demand that maximises profit.

Method 4: using gradients

At the point of profit maximisation, gradients of the total cost and total revenue curves are equal.

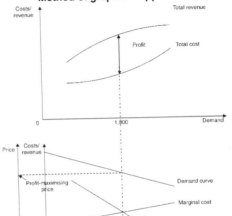

Method 3: graphical approach

Full cost plus pricing

The sales price is determined by calculating the full cost of the product and then adding a % mark-up for profit.

- An average profit mark-up can be used as a general guideline if prices must be quoted regularly to prospective customers.

- The mark-up does not have to be rigid and fixed but can be varied to suit the circumstances.

Problems

- The price must be adjusted to suit market and demand conditions.

- Output volume (a key factor in the determination of the overhead absorption rate) has to be budgeted.

- Suitable overhead absorption bases must be selected.

- Most importantly, full cost plus pricing fails to recognise that since demand may be determined by price, there will be a profit-maximising combination of price and demand.

A full cost determined by activity based costing as opposed to absorption costing might be more appropriate in today's business environment.

Marginal cost plus pricing / mark-up pricing

> Sales price = marginal cost of production (or marginal cost of sales) + profit margin

Pricing in a limiting factor situation

Suppose a business is working at full capacity and is restricted by a shortage of resources from expanding its output further. By deciding what target profit it would like to earn, it can establish a mark-up per unit of limiting factor.

Advantages of mark-up pricing

- ☑ Simple and easy
- ☑ Mark-up percentage can be varied to reflect demand conditions
- ☑ Helps create a better awareness of the concepts and implications of marginal cost and CVP analysis
- ☑ Used by businesses where there is a readily-identifiable basic variable cost (eg retail industries)

Drawbacks of mark-up pricing

- ☒ Does not ensure that sufficient attention is paid to demand conditions, competitors' prices and profit maximisation
- ☒ Ignores fixed overheads

Product bundling

Sell a number of products/services as a package at a price lower than the sum of their individual prices (eg hotel package includes use of leisure facilities).

Psychological pricing

Price a product at £9.99 instead of £10 or withdraw an unsuccessful product from the market and relaunch it at a higher price (customers perceiving lower price = lower quality).

Premium pricing

Make a product appear different to justify a premium price.

Multiple products and loss leaders

Charge a very low price for one product to make consumers buy additional products in the range which carry higher margins.

Pricing with optional extras

The pricing decision rests on whether the increase in sales revenue from the increased price that can be charged is greater than the increase in costs required to incorporate extra features.

Special orders

Use **minimum pricing** to price special orders (which arise if an organisation has spare capacity or it has no regular source of income and relies exclusively on its ability to respond to demand (eg building firm)).

Market penetration pricing

A policy of low prices when a product is first introduced in order to obtain sufficient penetration in the market

When to use

- To discourage new entrants into the market
- To shorten the initial period of the PLC
- If demand is highly elastic
- If significant economies of scale are possible with high output volumes

Market skimming

A policy of charging high prices when a product is first launched, and lower prices as it moves into later stages of the PLC

When to use

- If a product is new and different
- If strength of demand and price sensitivity are unknown
- If product differentiation is possible
- To make a quick profit if the PLC is short

Price discrimination

Price discrimination is the practice of charging different prices for the same product to different groups of buyers when these prices are not reflective of cost differences

Bases on which discriminating prices can be set

- By market segment (eg for students)
- By product version (eg 'add on extras' in cars)
- By place (eg theatre seats)
- By time (eg off-peak travel bargains)

'Own label' pricing is a form of price discrimination.

Product differentiation

This may be used to make products appear to be different. By segmenting markets, premium prices can then be justified in some market sectors.

Pricing to recover an investment

This is based on achieving a minimum payback period and should be used if the business is high risk, if rapid changes in fashion/technology are expected or if an innovator is short of cash.

Using discounts

Reasons

- To sell off seconds
- Normal practice (eg antiques trade)
- To get cash in quickly
- To get rid of perishable goods

4: Multi-product breakeven analysis

Topic List

Breakeven point

C/S ratio

Sales/product mix decisions

Target profits and margin of safety

Multi-product breakeven charts

Sensitivity analysis

You need to be completely confident of the aspects of breakeven analysis covered in your earlier studies.

*It is vital to remember that for multi-product breakeven analysis, a **constant product sales mix** (whenever x units of product A are sold, y units of product B and z units of product C are also sold) must be **assumed**.*

Key question to try in the kit:
Section A questions
RDF Ltd

Example (J Ltd) used throughout this chapter (where appropriate)

J Ltd produces and sells two products

- The M sells for £7 per unit and has a total variable cost of £3 per unit.
- The N sells for £15 per unit an.d has a total variable cost of £5 per unit.

For every five units of M sold, one unit of N will be sold.

Fixed costs total £30,000.

How to calculate a multi-product breakeven point

1. Calculate the contribution per unit.
2. Calculate the contribution per mix.
3. Calculate the breakeven point in number of mixes.
4. Calculate the breakeven point in units and revenue.

Example (J Ltd)

1. M = £4 N = £10
2. (£4 × 5) + (£10 × 1) = £30
3. Fixed costs ÷ contribution per mix = £30,000 ÷ £30 = 1,000 mixes
4. M 1,000 × 5 = 5,000 units
   5,000 × £7 = £35,000 revenue

   N 1,000 × 1 = 1,000 units
   1,000 × £15 = £15,000 revenue

   Total breakeven revenue = £50,000

How to calculate a multi-product C/S (or profit volume or P/V) ratio

Calculation of breakeven sales: approach 1

1 Calculate the revenue per mix.
2 Calculate the contribution per mix.
3 Calculate the average C/S ratio.
4 Calculate the total breakeven point.
5 Calculate the revenue ratio per mix.
6 Calculate the breakeven sales.

Example

1 $(£7 \times 5) + (£15 \times 1) = £50$

2 $(£4 \times 5) + (£10 \times 1) = £30$

3 $(£30 \div £50) \times 100\% = 60\%$

4 Fixed costs ÷ C/S ratio = £30,000 ÷ 0.6
= £50,000

5 $(£7 \times 5) : (£15 \times 1) = 35 : 15$ or $7 : 3$

6 M = £50,000 × 7/10 = £35,000
N = £50,000 × 3/10 = £15,000
£50,000

Calculation of breakeven sales: approach 2

You may just be provided with individual C/S ratios.

Example

C/S ratio of X = 45%
C/S ratio of Y = 35%
Ratio of sales = 3:4

$$\text{Average C/S ratio} = \frac{(45\% \times 3) + (35\% \times 4)}{7}$$

$$= 39.3\%$$

You can then carry on from step 4 on page 33.

Target contributions

Example (J Ltd)

J Ltd wishes to earn contribution of £500,000.

Sales revenue = (£1 ÷ C/S ratio) × £500,000
= (£1 ÷ 0.6*) × £500,000 = £833,333

* from example on page 33

Any change in the proportions of products in the mix will change the contribution per mix and the average C/S ratio and hence the breakeven point.

Most profitable mix option

Suppose J Ltd (from our example) has the option of changing the sales ratio to 2M to 4N. Which is the optimal mix?

1 Calculate breakeven point in number of mixes.

2 Calculate breakeven point in units and revenue.

Example (J Ltd)

1 Mix 1: 1,000 mixes (calculated on page 145)

Mix 2: Contribution per mix = (£4 × 2) + (£10 × 4)
= £48

Breakeven point = £30,000 ÷ £48
= 625 mixes

2 Mix 1: £50,000 (calculated on page 145)

Mix 2: M   625 × 2 = 1,250 units
1,250 × £7 = £8,750 units

N   625 × 4 = 2,500 units
2,500 × £15 = £37,500 revenue

Total breakeven revenue = £46,250

Mix 2 is preferable because it requires a lower level of sales to break even (because it has a higher average contribution per unit sold of £48/6 = £8 (compared with £30/6 = £5 for mix 1).

4: Multi-product breakeven analysis

Changing the product mix

ABC Ltd sells products Alpha and Beta in the ratio 5:1 at the same selling price per unit. Beta has a C/S ratio of 66.67% and the overall C/S ratio is 58.72%. How do we calculate the overall C/S ratio if the mix is changed to 2:5?

1 Calculate the missing C/S ratio

- Calculate original market share (Alpha 5/6, Beta 1/6).
- Calculate weighted C/S ratios.
  Beta: $0.6667 \times 0.1667 = 0.1111$
  Alpha: $0.5872 - 0.1111 = 0.4761$
- Calculate the missing C/S ratio.

	Alpha	Beta	Total
C/S ratio	0.5713 *	0.6667	
Market share	× 0.8333	× 0.1667	
	0.4761	0.1111	0.5872

* 0.4761/0.8333

2 Calculate the revised overall C/S ratio

	Alpha	Beta	Total
C/S ratio (as in 1)	0.5713	0.6667	
Market share (2/7:5/7)	× 0.2857	× 0.7143	
	0.1632	0.4762	0.6394

> The overall C/S ratio has increased because of the increase in the proportion of the mix of the Beta, which has the higher C/S ratio.

Target profits: approach 1

1 Calculate the contribution per mix.

2 Calculate the required number of mixes.

3 Calculate the required number of units and sales revenue of each product.

> You should remember from your earlier studies that the contribution required to earn a target profit (P) = fixed costs + P.

Example (J Ltd)

Suppose J Ltd wishes to earn profit of £24,900.

1 £30 (as on page 32)

2 (Fixed costs + required profit)/contribution per mix = £(30,000 + 24,900)/£30 = 1,830 mixes

	£
3 M: (1,830 × 5) units for (× £7)	64,050
N: (1,830 × 1) units for (× £15)	27,450
Total revenue	91,500
Variable costs (9,150 × £3) + (1,830 × £5)	36,600
Fixed costs	30,000
Profit	24,900

Target profits: approach 2

1 Calculate the average C/S ratio.
2 Calculate the required total revenue.

Example (J Ltd)

1 60% (from page 33)

2 Required contribution ÷ C/S ratio
= (fixed costs + profit) ÷ C/S ratio
= £54,900 ÷ 0.6 = £91,500

Margin of safety

1 Calculate the breakeven point in revenue.
2 Calculate the margin of safety.

Example (J Ltd)

Suppose J Ltd has budgeted sales of £62,000.

1 £50,000 (from page 32)

2 Budgeted sales – breakeven sales
= £(62,000 – 50,000) = £12,000
= 19.4% of budgeted sales

Breakeven chart

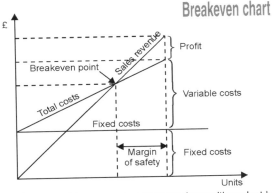

A multi-product breakeven chart can only be drawn on the assumption that the sales proportions are fixed.

There are three possible approaches to preparing multi-product breakeven charts.

- Output in £ sales and a constant product mix
- Products in sequence
- Output in tems of % of forecast sales and a constant product mix

P/V chart

Suppose J Ltd's sales budget is 6,000 units of M and 1,200 units of N.

Revenue (6,000 × £7 + 1,200 × £15) = £60,000

Variable costs (6,000 × £3 + 1,200 × £5) = £24,000

On the chart, products are shown individually, from left to right, in order of size of decreasing C/S ratio.

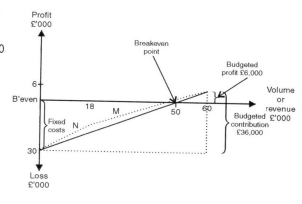

	C/S ratio	Cum sales £'000	Cum profit £'000
N	66.67%	18	*(18)
M	57.14%	60	6

* (1,200 × £15) – (12,000 × £5) – £30,000

- The overall company breakeven point

- Which products should be expanded in output (the most profitable in terms of C/S ratio) and which, if any, should be discontinued

- What effect changes in selling price and sales revenue would have on breakeven point and profit

- The average profit (the solid line which joins the two ends of the dotted line) earned from the sales of the products in the mix

Focuses on how a result will alter if estimates of variable values or underlying assumptions change. It can highlight the risks that an existing cost structure poses and so may lead managers to consider alternatives.

Sensitivity analysis and P/V charts

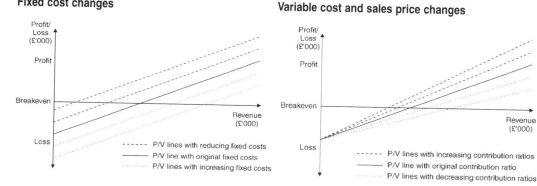

Fixed cost changes

Profit/Loss (£'000)

Profit

Breakeven

Revenue (£'000)

Loss

- - - - P/V lines with reducing fixed costs
——— P/V line with original fixed costs
········· P/V lines with increasing fixed costs

Variable cost and sales price changes

Profit/Loss (£'000)

Profit

Breakeven

Revenue (£'000)

Loss

- - - - P/V lines with increasing contribution ratios
——— P/V line with original contribution ratio
········· P/V lines with decreasing contribution ratios

Spreadsheets and Monte Carlo simulations may be required for complex situations.

5: Limiting factor analysis

Topic List

Decisions involving one limiting factor

Decisions involving restricted freedom of action

Make or buy decisions and scarce resources

Limiting factors and shadow prices

Assumptions and further considerations

A resource (such as labour or materials) which limits production to a level below demand is known as a limiting (or key) factor. It is assumed in limiting factor analysis (a technique for determining the optimum product mix) that management will select a profit-maximising product mix and that profit is maximised when contribution is maximised (given no change in fixed cost expenditure).

Key questions to try in the kit:
Section A questions
MN Ltd

Scenario	How to maximise contribution/profit	Detail
Sales demand restricts greater production/output	Make exactly the amount required for sales (and no more) provided that each product sold earns a positive contribution.	
One scarce resource (such as material or labour)	Earn the biggest possible contribution per unit of scarce resource (see example below).	Assume fixed costs remain unchanged whatever the production mix, the only relevant costs being variable costs.
One limiting factor and restrictions on sales demand	Rank products in order of contribution-earning ability per unit of limiting factor but produce the top-ranked products up to the sales demand limit.	Although there may appear to be more than one scarce resource, it may be that there is no limiting factor except sales demand or that there is only one scarce resource that prevents full potential sales demand being achieved.

An examination problem might present you with a situation in which there is a limiting factor, without specifically stating so, and you will have the task of recognising what the situation is. You may be given a hint with the wording of the question.

For example, an exam question once stated that 'it has been estimated that the consultants will be able to work for a total of 2,400 days during the year'.

If you suspect the existence of a limiting factor, some quick computations should confirm your suspicions.

1 Calculate the amount of the scarce resource (material quantities, labour hours, machine hours and so on) needed to meet the potential sales demand.

2 Calculate the amount of the scarce resource available (for example number of employees multiplied by maximum working hours per employee).

3 Compare the two figures. Obviously, if the resources needed exceed the resources available, there is a limiting factor on output and sales.

Example

L Ltd sells two products, the T and the J.

	T	J
	£	£
Direct labour (£5 per hour)	15	10
Direct materials (£2 per kg)	2	5
Variable overheads	2	2
Fixed overheads	3	3
	22	20
Selling price	£25	£24
Maximum demand	10,000	8,000
Maximum availability of labour		40,000 hrs

1 Confirm limiting factor is *not* sales.

Labour hours required to fulfil demand = (10,000 × 3) + (8,000 × 2) = 46,000, which means there is a shortfall of 6,000 hours.

2 Calculate the contribution per unit of scarce resource.

	T	J
Unit contribution	£(25 – 19) £6	£(24 – 17) £7
Labour hours per unit	3	2
Contribution per labour hour	£2	£3.50
Rank	2nd	1st

3 Work out budgeted production and sales.

Product	Hours	Production	Cont'n per unit £	Total cont'n £
J	(8,000 × 2) = 16,000	(÷ 2) 8,000	7	56,000
T	Balance = 24,000	(÷ 3) 8,000	6	48,000
	40,000			104,000

The profit-maximising product mix might not be possible because the mix is also restricted by a factor other than a scarce resource.

In such circumstances the organisation might have to produce more of a particular product or products than the level established by ranking according to contribution per unit of limiting factor.

Expect objective test questions on limiting factor analysis.

Factors that restrict freedom of action

- A contract to supply a certain number of products

- Provision of a complete product range and/or maintenance of customer goodwill

- Maintenance of a certain market share

Basic approach

1. Rank the products in the normal way.

2. Take account of the minimum production requirements within the optimum production plan.

3. Allocate the remaining resources according to the ranking.

Example

In the earlier example about L Ltd, suppose that the company has contracted to supply 9,000 units of T to an important customer. Here is the revised optimum sales/production plan.

Product	Hours	Production	Contribution per unit £	Total contribution £
T	(9,000 × 3) = 27,000	9,000	6	54,000
J	balance = 13,000	(13,000 ÷ 2) = 6,500	7	45,500
	40,000			99,500

An examination question is highly unlikely to tell you that an organisation has a 'restricted freedom of action'. Instead, look out for hints such as 'contracted to supply ...', 'minimum to be produced ...' and so on.

Suppose a company must subcontract work to make up a shortfall in its own production capacity.

Its total costs are minimised if those units bought have the lowest extra variable cost of buying per unit of scarce resource saved.

Example

A company, which makes three products, has limited labour time available.

	A	B	C
	£	£	£
Variable cost of making	10	16	14
Variable cost of buying	19	20	19
Extra variable cost of buying	9	4	5
Labour hours saved by buying (per unit)	3	2	2
Extra variable cost of buying per hour saved	£3	£2	£2.50
Priority for making in-house	1st	3rd	2nd

Opportunity cost

This represents the benefits foregone by using a limiting factor in one way instead of the next most profitable way.

Example

In the example on page 47, the opportunity cost of making J instead of more units of T is £2 per labour hour (T's contribution per labour hour).

If more labour hours were made available, more units of T (up to 10,000) would be made and an extra contribution of £2 per labour hour could be earned.

Similarly if fewer labour hours were available, fewer units of T would be made, production of J being kept at 8,000 units.

The loss of labour hours would cost the company £2 per labour hour in lost contribution.

Shadow price

A shadow price is the increase in contribution which would be created by having available one additional unit of a limiting resource at its normal variable cost.

This **lost contribution** (which is the marginal-earning potential of the limiting factor at the profit-maximising output level), is the **internal opportunity cost** or **shadow price** (or **dual price**) of the limiting factor.

5: Limiting factor analysis

Assumptions in limiting factor analysis

- Fixed costs will be the same whatever decision is taken.

- Unit variable costs are constant for all quantities of output.

- Sales demand is known with certainty.

- Resource requirements are known with certainty.

- Units of output are divisible.

Further considerations

- How much will sales demand be affected by changes in sales price, and how interdependent are sales of different products?

- Customer loyalty may be adversely affected by the business ceasing to produce a product.

- Competitors may take over vacated markets.

- It may not be possible to restart production of the product if labour skills have been lost.

- Further research may indicate the limiting factor is only limiting because of problems with the production process.

- Managers may want to achieve a satisfactory mix rather than a profit-maximising product mix in order to maintain employee goodwill.

Topic List

Linear programming is a technique for allocating scarce resources so as to maximise profit or minimise costs. It can be applied to problems with the following features.

- A **single objective** to maximise or minimise the value of a certain function

- **Several constraints**, typically scarce resources, that limit the value of the objective function

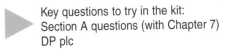

Key questions to try in the kit:
Section A questions (with Chapter 7)
DP plc

Linear programming

A technique for allocating scarce resources so as to maximise or minimise a range of numerical quantities (although most commonly to maximise contribution or minimise costs)

Which technique to use		
Number of products	**Number of scarce resources**	**Technique**
Any number	1	Limiting factor analysis
2	Any number	Graphical approach to linear programming
3 or more	Any number	Simplex approach to linear programming (covered in Chapter 7)

This example will be used throughout the chapter.

1 Define variables

- Let x = number of standard produced each month
- Let y = number of deluxe produced each month

2 Establish objective function

Maximise contribution (C) = 15x + 20y subject to the following constraints

3 Establish constraints

- Labour: $5x + 10y \leq 4,000$
- Material: $10x + 5y \leq 4,250$
- Non negativity: $x \geq 0, y \geq 0$

Students often have problems with constraints of the style 'the quantity of one type must not exceed twice that of the other'. This can be interpreted as follows: the quantity of one type (say X) must not exceed (must be less than or equal to) twice that of the other (2Y) (ie $X \leq 2Y$).

4 Graph the problem

- Labour: $5x + 10y = 4,000$; if $x = 0$, $y = 400$, and if $y = 0$, $x = 800$

- Material: $10x + 5y = 4,250$; if $x = 0$, $y = 850$, and if $y = 0$, $x = 425$

5 Define feasible area/region

This is the area where *all* inequalities are satisfied (area above x axis and y axis ($x \geq 0$, $y \geq 0$), below material constraint ($\leq$) *and* below labour constraint ($\leq$)).

> If you have to draw a graph make sure that it has a title, that the axes are labelled and that the constraint lines and feasible area are clearly identified.

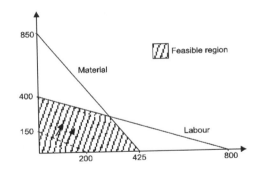

6: Linear programming (graphical)

6 Determine optimal solution

Method 1

- Add an iso-contribution line (suppose C = £3,000 so that if C = 15x + 20y, then if x = 0, y = 150, and if y = 0, x = 200).

- (Sliding your ruler across the page if necessary) find the point furthest from the origin but still in the feasible area.

- Use simultaneous equations to find out the x and y coordinates at the optimal solution, the intersection of the material and labour constraints (x = 300, y = 250)(or find them directly from the graph).

Method 2

- Determine all possible intersection points of constraints and axes using simultaneous equations.

- Calculate contribution at each intersection point to determine which is the optimal solution.

> If the iso-contribution line is exactly parallel to one of the constraint lines there will not be a single optimum solution, but a range of solutions along the part of the line within the feasible area.

Whatever the objective of the linear programming problem, the optimal solution is the one that yields the largest value for the objective function in the case of a maximisation problem, the lowest value in the case of a minimisation problem.

Minimisation problems

If the objective were to minimise costs the optimal solution would be at the point in the feasible area closest to the origin.

Slack and surplus

If a resource which has a maximum availability is not binding at the optimal solution, there will be slack.

If a minimum quantity of a resource must be used and, in the optimal solution, more than this quantity is used, there is a surplus on the minimum requirement.

6: Linear programming (graphical)

Shadow price

> The extra contribution or profit that may be earned by relaxing by one unit a binding resource constraint

- Shadow prices are calculated on the basis that the extra available resource costs the normal variable amount.

- Shadow prices represent the maximum premium above the normal variable amount that an organisation should be willing to pay for one extra unit of a resource.

- Since shadow prices indicate the effect of a one unit change in a constraint, they provide a measure of the sensitivity of a result.

- The shadow price of a constraint that is not binding at the optimal solution is zero.

- Shadow prices are only valid for a small range before the constraint becomes non-binding or different resources become critical.

- Shadow prices enable management to make better informed decisions about payment of overtime premium, bonuses, premiums on small orders of raw materials etc.

Sales price sensitivity analysis

Example

Suppose the sales price of the standard is reduced by £6 so that contribution becomes £9.

Now $C = 9x + 20y$

An iso-contribution line would now have a shallower slope parallel to, say, $9x + 20y = 1,800$.

This iso-contribution line would leave the feasible area at the intersection of the labour constraint and the y axis (0, 400).

If x's selling price reduces by £6, the optimal solution is to produce 400 units of y, but no units of x.

Limiting factor sensitivity analysis

Example

Suppose the availability of labour was reduced by one hour.

- The optimal solution would be at the intersection of $5x + 10y = 3,999$ and $10x + 5y = 4,250$.
- Solution by simultaneous equations now gives $x = 300.067$ units, $y = 249.867$ units.

	£
Profit with original constraints	
$((15 \times 300) + (20 \times 250))$	9,500
Revised profit $((15 \times 300.067) + (20 \times 249.867))$	9,498
Reduction in contribution from loss of one labour hour	2

- Shadow price of one hour of labour = £2
- Profit would increase by £2 if an additional labour hour was made available (assuming the additional labour cost the normal variable cost) as long as labour is a limiting factor.
- Labour would cease to be a limiting factor when the labour constraint passes through the intersection of the material constraint and the y axis (0, 850) ie when availability $(5x + 10y) = (5 \times 0) + (10 \times 850)$
$$= 8,500 \text{ hours.}$$

7: Linear programming (simplex)

Topic List

Formulating the problem

Interpretation of the final tableau

Sensitivity analysis

Using linear programming

The simplex method is a method of solving linear programming problems with two or more decision variables.

Key questions to try in the kit:
Section A questions (with Chapter 6)
Small car vacuum cleaner I and II
Fertiliser II
Venture capital company

Six steps to formulating the problem

1 Define variables

Let x = number of product X produced each month

Let y = number of product Y produced each month

2 Establish objective function

For example, maximise contribution (C) = $20x + 16y$ subject to the following constraints.

3 Establish constraints

For example:

> In the exam you need to be able to formulate the problem and interpret the final tableau.

Materials	$5x + 2y \leq 3,000$
Labour	$x + 3y \leq 1,750$
Machine time	$3x + 2y \leq 2,100$
Non negativity	

4 Introduce slack variables

> A slack variable represents the amount of a constraining resource or item that is unused. One is required for each non-negativity constraint.

Let a = quantity of unused materials
    b = number of unused labour hours ■————————■
    c = number of unused machine hours

The slack variables a, b, c will be equal to 0 in the final solution only if the combined production of x and y uses up all the available materials, labour and machine time.

5 Redefine constraints

$5x + 2y + a = 3{,}000$
$x + 3y + b = 1{,}750$
$3x + 2y + c = 2{,}100$

6 Redefine objective function

- Express it as an equation with the right hand side equal to zero.
- Insert the slack variables but with zero coefficients

Maximise contribution (C) given by $C - 20x - 16y + 0a + 0b + 0c = 0$

Here is the optimal solution for the example detailed in Steps 1 to 6.

Example

Variables in solution	x	y	a	b	c	Solution column
x	1	0	0	−0.29	0.43	400
a	0	0	1	0.59	−1.87	100
y	0	1	0	0.43	−0.14	450
Solution row	0	0	0	1.08	6.36	15,200

- The solution is optimal because the shadow prices in the bottom row are all positive.
- Make and sell 400 units of X and 450 of Y to earn contribution of £15,200.
- 100 units of material will be unused.

- All labour and machine time will be used.
- The shadow price of labour time (b) is £1.08 (the amount by which contribution would increase if more labour time could be made available at its normal variable cost).
- The shadow price of materials is nil.

Look back at the final tableau on page 66.

Having more or less of a scarce resource

The figures in the (b) column provide the following information for each extra labour hour that is available.

- Contribution would increase by £1.08.
- 0.29 units less of X would be made, losing contribution of 0.29 × 20 = £5.80.
- The value of (a) unused materials would increase by 0.59 units.
- 0.43 units more of Y would be made, increasing contribution by 0.43 × 16 = £6.88.

- The net increase in contribution = £(6.88 − 5.80) = £1.08.
- The limit to the number of extra labour hours that would earn an extra £1.08 = 400 (x in the optimal tableau) ÷ 0.29 (the reduction in x for each extra labour hour)) = 1,379.3 hours, so that the shadow price is only valid up to a total limit of 1,750 + 1,379.3 = 3,129.3 hours.

Obtaining extra resources at a premium on cost

It would not be worth obtaining extra labour via overtime working at time and a half (say £2 per hour premium) as this is greater than the extra contribution of £1.08 per hour.

7: Linear programming (simplex)

Using computer packages

Typical output from a computer package

Objective function (c)

Interpretation

270,000 —— Total optimal contribution is £270,000.

Variable	Value	Relative loss
x	20	0.00
y	130	0.00
z	0	75.00

If one unit of Z were made, total contribution would fall by £75.

Constraint	Slack/surplus	Worth
1 (≤)	90.00	0.00
2 (≤)	0.00	50.00
3 (limit on y)	0.00	250.00
4 (minimum X (1))	19.00	0.00

Slack = 90 means 90 units of resource 1 unused.

Slack = 0 means all resource 2 is used. Contribution would increase by £50 for each unit of resource 2 made available.

Slack = 0 means limit has been met. Contribution would increase by £250 if the limit on Y could be raised by 1.

Surplus = 19 means (19 + 1) units of X made.

To maximise contribution produce 20 units of X and 130 units of Y.

- In general any constraint with a slack of zero has a positive worth figure, while any constraint with a positive slack figure will have a worth of zero.

- In general, only those decision variables with a relative loss of zero will have a positive value in the optimal solution.

In the exam you may be provided with output from a computer package for linear programming similar to that below.

Variables

A	50
B	30

Constraints

N1	3,000	
N2		5
N3		4

Contribution   £100,000

To check the meaning of the figures, you could calculate the usage of resource N1 given production of 50 A and 30 B. If the difference between availability and usage of N1 is 3000, you would then know that £5 and £4 were shadow prices.

Further assumptions (in addition to those which apply to limiting factor analysis)

- The total amount of each scare resource is known with certainty.
- There is no interdependence between the demand for different products.

Uses

- Selling different products
- Calculation of relevant costs
- Maximum payment for additional scarce resources
- Budgeting
- Control
- Capital budgeting

Practical difficulties

- The identification of resources in short supply and their availability is problematic.
- Management may opt for a 'satisfactory' product mix rather than one that is profit maximising.
- The assumption of linearity may be totally invalid. For example the learning effect may be relevant.
- The model is essential static.
- Variables can only take on integer values.
- The shadow price only applies up to a certain limit.

8: Investment decision making

Capital expenditure differs from day to day revenue expenditure because it often involves a bigger outlay and the benefits from it are likely to accrue over a long period of time. Any proposed capital expenditure should therefore be properly appraised and found to be worthwhile before the decision is taken to go ahead with the expenditure.

Key questions to try in the kit:
Section A questions (with Chapter 9)
Intranet II

Investment decision-making process

1 Origination of proposals

Set up a mechanism which scans the environment for potential opportunities and provides an early warning of future problems.

2 Project screening

Carry out a qualitative evaluation:

- Purpose
- 'Fit' with long-term objectives
- Resources required and their availability
- Risk
- Time frame
- Key success factors
- Alternatives

3 Analysis and acceptance

- Submit standard format financial information as a formal investment proposal.
- Classify the project by type.
- Carry out **financial analysis.**
- Compare the outcome of the analysis to predetermined acceptance criteria.
- Consider the project in the light of current and future capital budgets.
- Make the **go/no go decision.**
- Monitor the progress of the project.

4 Monitor progress

- Control over excess spending
  - The authority to make capital expenditure decisions should be formally assigned.
  - Capital expenditure decisions should be documented and properly approved.
  - If actual expenditure exceeds the amount authorised by a permitted percentage, re-authorisation should be required.
  - Authorisation of any capital expenditure which would take total spending above the total capital budget should be referred to board level, for example, for approval.

- Control over delays
  - If capital expenditure has not taken place before a stated deadline is reached, the project should be resubmitted for fresh authorisation.
  - The proposer should be asked to explain reasons for the delay.

- Control over anticipated benefits
  - Ensure anticipated benefits do actually materialise, benefits are as big as anticipated and running costs do not exceed expectation.
  - The difficulty in controlling projects, however, is that they are usually 'unique', with no standard or yardstick against which to judge them.

Post audit

'An objective and independent appraisal of the measure of success of a capital expenditure project in progressing the business as planned. The appraisal should cover the implementation of the project from authorisation to commissioning and its technical and commercial performance after commissioning. The information provided is also used by management as feedback which aids the implementation and control of future projects.'

(Official Terminology)

Question 1: Why?

- The threat of post audit will motivate managers to work to achieve the project benefits promised.
- If carried out before the end of the project life it can improve efficiency/increase benefits or highlight those projects which should be discontinued.
- It can help to identify those managers who have been good/bad performers.
- Weaknesses in forecasting/estimating techniques may be identified.

Question 2: Which?

- Managers should perceive that every project has the chance of being audited.
- A reasonable guideline might be to audit all projects above a certain size and a random selection of smaller projects.
- A post audit should concentrate on those aspects of an investment which have been identified as particularly sensitive/critical to the success of the project.
- Consider cost/benefit trade-off.

Question 3: When?

An audit should not be carried out too soon (information is incomplete) or too late (management action is delayed and the usefulness of information reduced).

Problems

- Impact of uncontrollable factors
- Difficulty in separating costs and benefits
- Costly and time consuming
- If applied punitively, managers may become over cautious/risk averse
- Difficulty in identifying long-term strategic effects of projects

Alternative control processes

- Teams could manage a project from beginning to end.
- More time could be spent choosing projects.

Payback

> The time it takes the cash inflows ($\approx$ profits before depreciation) for an investment to equal the cash outflows, usually expressed in years

It is often used as a first screening method, the project being evaluated with a more sophisticated technique if it gets through the payback test.

Decision rules

1 When deciding between two or more competing projects, the usual decision is to accept the one with the shortest payback.

2 Reject a project if its payback is greater than a target payback.

Disadvantages

- ☒ It ignores the timing of cash flows within the payback period, the cash flows after the end of the payback period and hence the total project return.
- ☒ It ignores the time value of money.
- ☒ It makes no distinction between different projects with the same payback period.
- ☒ The choice of cut-off payback period is arbitrary.
- ☒ The method may lead to excessive investment in short-term projects.
- ☒ It takes account of the risk associated with the timing of cash flows but not the variability of those cash flows.

Advantages

- ☑ Long payback means capital is tied up.
- ☑ A focus on early payback can enhance liquidity.
- ☑ Investment risk is increased if payback is longer.
- ☑ Shorter-term forecasts are likely to be more reliable.
- ☑ The calculation is quick and simple.
- ☑ Payback is an easily understood concept.

Accounting rate of return (ARR)

There are several definitions of ARR (the method selected should be used consistently) but the recommended definition is

$$ARR = \frac{\text{Average annual profits from an investment}}{\text{Average investment}} \times 100\%$$

- Annual profits are after depreciation
- Average investment = ½(initial cost − residual value)

If you are not provided with a figure for profit, assume that net cash inflow minus depreciation equals profit.

Decision rules

- *One* project
  - □ If the ARR is greater than the target rate of return, accept the project.
  - □ If the ARR is less than the target rate of return, reject the project.

- When comparing *two or more mutually exclusive projects*, the project with the highest ARR should be chosen (provided the ARR is greater than the target ARR).

Advantages

- ☑ Quick and simple
- ☑ Looks at the entire project life
- ☑ Easily calculated from financial statements

Disadvantages

- ☒ Takes no account of the timing of cash flows
- ☒ Based on accounting profits which are subject to a number of different accounting treatments
- ☒ Takes no account of the size of the investment or the length of the project
- ☒ Ignores the time value of money

Example

Equipment J has a capital cost of £100,000 and a disposal value of £20,000 at the end of its five-year life. Profits before depreciation over the five years total £150,000.

∴ Total profit after depreciation = £(150,000 – 80,000) = £70,000

Average annual profit after depreciation = £14,000

(Capital cost + disposal cost) / 2 = £60,000

ARR = (14/70) × 100% = 20%

9: DCF techniques

Topic List

Net present value (NPV) method

Internal rate of return (IRR) method

DCF: additional points

DCF techniques and their applications were examined on many occasions under the previous syllabus version of this paper. This is therefore one of the key chapters.

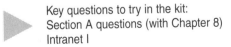

Key questions to try in the kit:
Section A questions (with Chapter 8)
Intranet I

Present value

The cash equivalent now (X) of a sum of money (V) receivable or payable at the end of n time periods

Discounting provides the formula $X = V/(1+r)^n$, where r is the rate of return.

Net present value

The value obtained by discounting all cash inflows and outflows of a capital investment project by a chosen target rate of return

The NPV is based on cash flows of a project, not accounting profits.

Decision rules

- *One* project
  - If NPV > 0 ➜ accept project
  - If NPV < 0 ➜ reject project

- When comparing *two or more mutually exclusive projects*, the project with the highest positive NPV should be selected.

Assumptions in the NPV model

- Forecasts are certain.

- Information is freely available and costless.

- The discount rate is a measure of the opportunity cost of funds which ensures wealth maximisation for *all* individuals and companies.

Discount factors

Present value tables cover integer costs of capital from 1% to 20% for 1 to 20 years. If you require a discount factor for a non-integer interest rate (say 12.5%) or a period of time greater than 20 years, use $1/(1+r)^n$, where r = cost of capital and n = number of years.

Timing of cash flows

- A cash outlay to be incurred at the beginning of an investment project ('**now**') occurs at time 0 and will have a present value = outlay (since PV of £1 now = £1).

- A cash flow occurring **during the course of a time period** is assumed to occur at the end of the time period.

- A cash flow occurring **at the beginning of a time period** is assumed to occur at the end of the previous time period.

Perpetuities

An annual cash flow in perpetuity

The PV of £1 pa in perpetuity at r% = £1/r (where r is a decimal).

Net terminal value (NTV)

The cash surplus remaining at the end of a project after taking account of interest and capital repayments

The NTV discounted at the cost of capital = NPV

Annuities

A constant annual cash flow from year to year

Use discount factors from **cumulative present value tables.**

Example

PV of £1,000 in years 2 to 6 at a rate of r% =

$$£1,000 \times \begin{cases} \text{PV of £1 pa for yrs 1–6 at r\%} = & X \\ \text{PV of £1 pa for yrs 1–2 at r\%} = & \underline{(X)} \\ \text{PV of £1 pa for yrs 2–6 at r\%} = & \underline{\underline{X}} \end{cases}$$

IRR

The rate of interest at which the NPV of an investment is zero

Decision rule

If the IRR is greater than the target rate of return, the project is worth undertaking.

IRR of a perpetuity

- IRR = perpetuity ÷ initial investment

IRR of an annuity

- Cumulative PV factor for years 1 to n at rate r = initial investment ÷ annuity = X
- Look in cumulative PV tables along line for year n to find discount factor corresponding to X
- Corresponding rate = IRR

Example

An investment now of £300,000 will produce inflows of £80,000 per annum over the next five years. To find the IRR:

£300,000 = PV of £80,000 for years 1-5 at rate r

∴ £300,000 = (cumulative PV factor for years 1-5 at rate r) × £80,000

∴ 3.75 = cumulative PV factor for years 1 to 5 at rate r

Find 3.75 in the row for year 5. The corresponding rate is the IRR.

Interpolation method

Remember you will need to account for depreciation and any residual value when determining the ARR.

1 Calculate the NPV using a rough indicator of the IRR ($^2/_3$ (or $^3/_4$) × ARR).

2 If the resulting NPV > 0, recalculate the NPV using a higher rate.

3 If the resulting NPV < 0, recalculate the NPV using a lower rate.

The closer these NPVs are to zero, the closer the estimate to the true IRR.

4 $IRR = A + \left[\dfrac{P}{P+N} \times (B-A) \right]\%$

where

A = (lower) rate of return with positive NPV
B = (higher) rate of return with negative NPV
P = amount of positive NPV
N = absolute value of negative NPV

If P = £1,000 and N = −£2,000, P + N = £(1,000 + 2,000) = £3,000

Graphical approach

Suppose a project has the following NPVs at the
following discount rates.

Discount rate	NPV
%	£
5	5,300
10	2,900
15	(1,700)
20	(3,200)

These can be easily plotted on a graph.

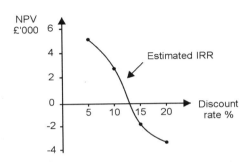

Recalculate the NPV using the estimated IRR (from the graph) of 13% and if the resulting NPV is not equal to, or very near, zero, additional NPVs at different discount rates should be calculated, the graph redrawn and a more accurate IRR determined.

NPV versus IRR

Which is better?

	NPV	IRR
When cash flow patterns are conventional both methods give the same accept or reject decision.	☑	☑
The IRR method is more easily understood.		☑
IRR and ROCE/ROI can be confused.	☑	
IRR ignores the relative sizes of investments.	☑	
When cash flow patterns are non-conventional there may be several IRRs of which decision makers must be aware to avoid making the wrong decision.	☑	
The NPV method is superior for ranking mutually exclusive projects in order of attractiveness.	☑	
When discount rates are expected to differ over the life of the project, such variations can be incorporated easily into NPV calculations but not into IRR calculations.	☑	

Despite the advantages of the NPV method over the IRR method, the IRR method is widely used in practice.

Time value of money

Why is £1 now worth more than £1 in the future?

- Uncertainty
- Inflation
- More weight is attached to current pleasures than to those occurring in the future

Project abandonment

A project should be abandoned if it becomes apparent that the present value of the net expected proceeds from abandonment are greater than the present value of the net expected proceeds from continuing the project.

You may need to incorporate the use of decision trees.

Costs to include in project appraisal

The cash flows to consider are the **relevant costs** of the project and could include extra taxation, residual value/disposal value of equipment or its disposal cost and changes in working capital.

Finance-related cash flows are normally excluded: they are only relevant if they incur a different rate of interest from the discount rate.

Examples of possible complications

- Outcomes in year N determine outcomes in year N + 1, year N + 2 etc
- Buy-back clause
- Events not anticipated at the outset

Discounted payback

This is the time it will take before a project's cumulative NPV turns from being negative to being positive.

The **discounted payback index (DPBI) or payback index** (sum of net discounted cash inflows ÷ initial cash outlay) is a measure of the number of times a project recovers the initial funds invested, which is important if funds are scarce.

Advantages of DCF method

- The time value of money is taken into account.
- The method uses all cash flows relating to the project.
- It allows for the timings of cash flows.
- There are universally accepted methods of calculating the NPV and IRR.

10: Further aspects of investment decision making

Topic List

Unequal lives and asset replacement

Capital rationing

Sensitivity analysis

For Paper P2, you need to extend your knowledge of investment decision making beyond both that covered in your earlier studies and the basics in Chapters 8 and 9 to more complex areas. You are far more likely to encounter a long question on sensitivity analysis than a question requiring you to carry out a simple DCF appraisal.

Key questions to try in the kit:
Section A questions
A2Z plc
NP plc
Healthcare organisation

Annualised equivalents

Enable a comparison to be made between NPVs of projects with different durations

$$= \frac{\text{NPV at } r\%}{\text{Cumulative } r\% \text{ discount factor for life of project}}$$

Decision rule

Choose the project with the higher annualised equivalent.

Replacement theory

(Identical replacement (how frequently))

1   Calculate the PV of costs for each replacement cycle over one cycle only.

2   Turn these PVs of costs into **equivalent annual costs**: $$\frac{\text{PV of cost over one replacement cycle}}{\text{Cumulative PV factor for number of years in cycle}}$$

3   The **optimum** replacement cycle is the one with the **lowest** equivalent annual cost.

Non-identical replacement (when)

The best time to replace an existing machine will be the option which gives the lowest NPV of cost in perpetuity, for both the existing machine and the machine which eventually replaces it.

1   Calculate optimum replacement cycle for new machine and its equivalent annual cost (as detailed above).

2   PV of cost in perpetuity of new machine from start of year when it is eventually purchased =

$$\frac{\text{equivalent annual cost}}{r} \qquad \text{where } r = \text{cost of capital}$$

3   For each replacement option, discount to time 0 the PV of cost in perpetuity of the new machine and the costs associated with the existing machine (such as relevant running costs and resale value which are dependant upon when it is replaced) by the appropriate discount factor.

4   Choose the option with the lowest PV of cost in perpetuity.

Capital rationing

If an organisation is in a capital rationing situation, it will not be able to proceed with all projects with positive NPVs because there is not enough capital for all of the investments.

Soft capital rationing is brought about by internal factors, **hard capital rationing** by external factors.

Basic approach

Rank projects in terms of the *profitability index (PI)* =

$$\frac{\text{PV of project's future cash flows}}{\text{PV of total capital outlays}}$$

Problems with PI method

- It can only be utilised if the projects are divisible.
- The selection takes no account of the strategic value of individual investments in the context of the organisation's objectives.
- It takes no account of cash flow patterns.
- It ignores the absolute size of individual investments.

Key assumptions

- Rationing occurs in a single period.
- Projects cannot be postponed.
- Risk does not impact on project choice.
- Projects are divisible.

Project	Investment £'000	PV of inflows £'000	NPV £'000	Ranking per NPV	PI	Ranking per PI
A	100	145	45	2	1.45	2
B	120	168	48	1	1.40	3
C	70	105	35	3	1.50	1

If £200,000 of capital is available, projects C and A should be accepted and ((200 – 170) ÷ 120) × 100%) 25% of project B.

Resulting NPV = £1,000(35 + 45 + (25% × 48)) = £92,000

Ranking on the basis of NPV would have resulted in an NPV £1,000(48 + ($^{80}/_{100}$ × 45)) = £84,000

Always rank on the basis of PI, not NPV.

When capital rationing occurs in a number of periods and two projects are under consideration, the graphical approach to linear programming is used to arrive at an NPV-maximising mix of products. If there are three or more projects the simplex method should be applied.

Sensitivity analysis is one method of analysing the risk surrounding a capital expenditure project. It enables an assessment to be made of how responsive the project's NPV is to changes in the variables used to calculate that NPV, which could include estimated selling price, initial cost, cost of capital, length of project, costs and benefits.

Margin of error approach

1 Calculate the project's NPV.

2 Determine the extent to which key variables may change before the investment results in a negative NPV.

Weaknesses

- The method requires that key variables are considered in isolation which is unrealistic since they are often interdependent.

- It does not examine the probability that any particular variation in costs/revenues might occur.

The sensitivity of an NPV computation to changes in a variable that affects the cashflows is:

$$\frac{\text{NPV of project}}{\text{PV of cashflow affected}} \times 100\%$$

Example

Year	Discount factor 8%	PV of plant cost £	PV of running costs £	PV of savings £	PV of net cash flow £
0	1.000	(7,000)			(7,000)
1	0.926		(1,852)	5,556	3,704
2	0.857		(2,143)	5,999	3,856
		(7,000)	(3,995)	11,555	560

Changes in cash flows which would need to occur for the project to break even (NPV = 0) are as follows.

- Plant costs would need to increase by a PV of £560 = 560/7,000 × 100% = 8%
- Running costs would need to increase by a PV of £560 = 560/3,995 × 100% = 14%
- Savings would need to fall by a PV of £560 = 560/11,555 × 100% = 4.8%

Management should review the estimates of benefits to asses whether or not there is a strong possibility of events occurring which would lead to a negative NPV (the PV of benefits only needs to drop by 4.8% before this happens) and, if the decision is taken to accept the investment, they should pay particular attention to controlling the benefits arising from the project.

Diagrammatic approach

With the key variable on the horizontal axis, plot a graph to show how a project's NPV (on the vertical axis) changes with changes in the key variable or to compare how sensitive the NPVs of two or more projects are to changes in the key variable. Straight lines can be plotted to approximate to curvilinear behaviour.

10: Further aspects of investment decision making

11: Taxation and inflation

Topic List

Allowing for inflation

Allowing for taxation

Remember that you are highly unlikely to get straightforward NPV calculations in the Paper P2 exam. Expect complexities such as inflation and taxation to be thrown in.

Key questions to try in the kit:
Section A questions
AB plc
PK Glass plc

Expressed in terms of the value of the £ at time 0   **Real cash flows**   **Real discount rate** ➤ The return required if there were no inflation

discount at

Expressed in terms of the actual amounts of money received in the future   **Money cash flows**   **Money discount rate** ➤ The return required given that inflation will occur

If various costs and benefits do not rise in line with the general level of inflation, apply the money rate to inflated values to determine an NPV.

> **Learn how the two rates are linked!**
>
> $(1 + \text{money rate}) = (1 + \text{real rate}) \times (1 + \text{inflation rate})$

Corporation tax

In the UK, under the system being introduced, corporation tax is payable by companies quarterly.

- In the seventh and tenth months of the year in which the profit is earned
- In the first and fourth months of the following year

Half the tax is therefore payable in the year in which the profits are earned and half in the following year.

When taxation is included in DCF calculations, use a post-tax required rate of return.

Example

If a project increases taxable profits by £5,000 in year 4, there will be tax payments of £5,000 × 30% × 50% = £750 in both year 4 and year 5 (assuming a tax rate of 30%).

These tax payments of £750 (a direct result of the project) need to be included in any DCF analysis.

Net cash flows from a project should be considered as the taxable profits arising from a project (unless given an indication to the contrary).

Capital allowances/WDAs

- WDAs reduce taxable profits and hence the tax payable.

- The rate at which WDAs are given will always be provided in the question but it is likely to be 25% on a reducing balance basis.

- The reduction in tax payable (to be included in any DCF analysis) = amount of WDA × tax rate.

- The benefit of WDAs are felt half in the year to which they relate and half in the following year.

> It maybe possible to claim WDAs on the costs of installation as well as original capital costs.

Example

A company purchases a machine costing £80,000. The rate of corporation tax is 30% and WDAs are given on a 25% reducing balance basis.

In year 2, WDA = (£80,000 × 75%) × 25% = £15,000

Tax saved = £15,000 × 30% = £4,500

Benefit received of 50% × £4,500 = £2,250 in both year 2 and year 3

Balancing allowances/charges

When plant is sold there will be a difference between the sales price and the reducing balance amount at the time of sale.

- Sales price > reducing balance
  → taxable profit (balancing charge)

- Sales price < reducing balance
  → tax allowable loss (balancing allowance)

> ### Example
>
> A machine has a written down value at the start of year 4 of £15,000. The corporation tax rate is 30%.
>
> - If it is sold for £10,000, there is a balancing allowance of £5,000 which is set against year 4 taxable profits, resulting in a reduction in tax paid of £5,000 × 30% = £1,500, the benefit of which will be received half in year 4 and half in year 5.
>
> - If it is sold for £20,000, the balancing charge of £5,000 will be included in year 4 taxable profits, and tax paid in each of years 4 and 5 will increase by £750.

The balancing allowance/charge should be dealt with in the year of sale.

Taxation and DCF appraisal

1.   Calculate **WDAs** and any **balancing allowance/charge.**

2.   Based on the WDAs and balancing allowance/charge calculated above, work out the **tax savings** (30% × WDA or allowance) and **tax increase** (30% × charge). These will **affect two years**, the year in which the allowance is claimed or charge occurs and the following year.

3.   Calculate the **extra tax** payable **due to savings** related to the project (saving × 30% × 50% in both the year of saving and the following year).

4.   Calculate the **tax savings due to non-capital costs** related to the project (cost × 30% × 50% in both the year in which the cost is incurred and the following year).

5.   Determine the project's **NPV**, including in the calculation capital cash flows, costs and savings related to the project, taxes on savings and any balancing charge and tax saved on WDAs, any balancing allowances and project costs.

12: Risk and uncertainty

Topic List

Risk and uncertainty

Probability

Sensitivity analysis

Decision trees

Value of information

Simulation models

This chapter covers some of the techniques that the management accountant can use to take account of any risk or uncertainty surrounding decisions. Topics covered here lend themselves particularly well to objective testing.

Key questions to try in the kit:
Section A questions
Holiday resort
Ice cream manufacturer
Pharmacy

Risk

Involves situations or events which may or may not occur, but whose probability of occurrence can be calculated statistically and the frequency of their occurrence predicted from past records

Uncertainty

Involves events whose outcome *cannot* be predicted with statistical confidence

An event will be risky or uncertain depending on whether or not sufficient information is available to allow the lack of certainty to be quantified. As a rule, however, the terms are used interchangeably.

Attitude to risk

Risk seeker   A decision maker interested in the best outcomes no matter how small the chance that they may occur

Risk neutral   A decision maker concerned with what will be the most likely outcome

Risk averse   A decision maker who acts on the assumption that the worst outcome might occur

The risk of a particular course of action should be considered in the context of the overall 'portfolio' of strategies adopted by an organisation.

Expected values (EV)

The EV of an opportunity is equal to the sum of (the probability of an outcome occurring × the return expected if it does occur) = Σpx (where p = probability of an outcome occurring and x = value of that outcome).

The calculation of EVs is more useful as a decision-making technique when outcomes will occur many times over (for example, the calculation of expected sales levels on the basis of sales levels over 360 previous days) rather than when a decision must be made once only (such as an investment decision based on a 70% chance of a profit of £50,000 and a 30% chance of a loss of £70,000).

Example

If contribution could be £10,000, £20,000 or £30,000 with respective probabilities of 0.3, 0.5 and 0.2, the EV of contribution =

	£
£10,000 × 0.3	3,000
£20,000 × 0.5	10,000
£30,000 × 0.2	6,000
EV of contribution	19,000

There may be further additional conditions, for example there may be only a 75% chance of making one of these three positive contributions and a 25% chance of a negative contribution of £10,000, in which case the EV = (£19,000 (calculation above) × 0.75) − (£10,000 × 0.25) = £14,250 − £2,500 = £11,750.

Bayes' strategy

When faced with a number of alternative decisions each with a range of possible outcomes, the optimum decision will be the one which gives the highest EV.

Cumulative probabilities

In the example opposite the cumulative probability that, say, total cost will be less than £10,000 is the sum of the combined probabilities for any total cost figure below £10,000 = 0.3 + 0.45 + 0.1 = 0.85.

Joint/combined probabilities

Example

If there is a 40% chance that costs will be £8 and a 75% probability that sales will be 500 units, the joint/combined probability of these two events is $0.4 \times 0.75 = 0.3$ and if other probabilities are £10 (60%) and 1,000 units (25%), the information can be tabulated as follows.

Volume	Prob	Cost	Prob	Combined prob	Total cost £	EV of total cost £
500	0.75	£8	0.4	0.30	4,000	1,200
		£10	0.6	0.45	5,000	2,250
1,000	0.25	£8	0.4	0.10	8,000	800
		£10	0.6	0.15	10,000	1,500
				1.00		5,750

Data tables

One-way/two-way data tables show the effects of a range of values of one/two variables.

	A	B	C	D
1	Price	£10.00		
2	Cost	£5.00		
3	Volume	1,000 units		
4				
5		£		
6	Sales	10,000		
7	Costs	(5,000)		
8	Profit	5,000		
9				
10	=B8	750	1,000	1,250
11	8	2,250	3,000	3,750
12	10	3,750	5,000	6,250
13	12	5.250	7,000	8,750
14				

Example

The spreadsheet shows an input section (cells A1 to B3), a combined calculation and output section (cells A6 to B8), and a two-way data table showing the profit earned at different combinations of sales volume (cells B10 to D10) and price (cells A11 to A13) (eg 750 x £(8 – 5) = £2,250).

Probability analysis and long-term decisions

Instead of using point estimates or 'most likely' figures, full probability distributions of variables can be drawn up.

Two approaches are then possible.

- Calculate EVs of variables and incorporate them into one NPV calculation.
- Calculate a number of NPVs using each of the options provided in the probability distribution and then calculate an EV of the NPVs.

Maximin basis for decision making

This is a 'play it safe' approach and involves choosing the option which has the 'best' worst result.

Using the standard deviation to measure risk

Risk can be measured by the possible variations of outcomes around the EV using the standard deviation, s

$$s = \sqrt{\Sigma p(x - \overline{x})^2}$$

where $\overline{x}$ is the EV of the variable in question, x is each possible value of the variable and p is the probability of each possible variable value.

Risks can be compared using the coefficient of variation (s ÷ EV of variable in question).

Example

	Project B	Projet W
Standard deviation	£10,000	£104,600
EV of profit	£73,900	£91,200
Coefficient of variation	0.14	1.15

Histograms and probability distributions

A frequency distribution can be represented by a histogram.

The graph of a probability distribution is the same as the associated histogram, but with the vertical axis marked in proportions, not numbers.

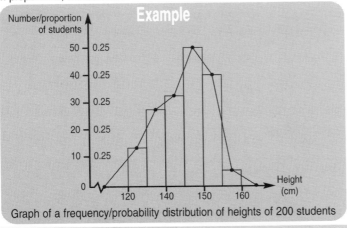

- The area under the curve of a frequncy distribution represents the total number of items in the population.

- The area under the curve of a probability distribution is 100% or 1.

Graph of a frequency/probability distribution of heights of 200 students

The essence of all approaches to sensitivity analysis is to carry out calculations with one set of values for the variables and then substitute other possible values for the variables to see how this effects the overall outcome.

Approach 3

Estimate by how much a variable would need to differ before a decision maker was indifferent between two options.

Approach 1
Estimate by how much a variable would need to differ from its estimated value before the decision would change (see Chapter 10).

Approach 2
Estimate whether a decision would change if a variable was X% higher than expected.

Sensitivity analysis is one form of 'what-if?' analysis

Example

Option 2 is £10,000 more expensive than option 1 and involves taking a discount of 10% from a supplier from whom you purchase £50,000 of goods (before discount) pa for 4 years. Ignore the time value of money. Discount needs to be £10,000 (difference) + £20,000 (current discount) if option 2 is as good as option 1.

$\therefore (4 \times £50,000) \times X\% = £30,000$

$\therefore X = 15\%$ (rate at which you are indifferent between the two options)

Preparation

1 Start with a (labelled) **decision point.**

2 Add branches for each option/alternative.

3 If the outcome of an option is 100% certain, the branch for that alternative is complete.

4 If the outcome of an option is uncertain (because they are a number of possible outcomes), add an **outcome point.**

5 For each possible outcome, add a branch (with the relevant probability) to the outcome point.

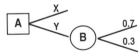

6 Always work **chronologically** from **left to right.**

Evaluating the decision

Work from **right to left** and calculate the EV of revenue/cost/contribution/profit at each outcome point (**rollback analysis**).

Example

As a result of an increase in demand for a town's car parking facilities, the owners of a car park are reviewing their business operations. A decision has to be made now to select one of the following three options for the next year.

Option 1: Make no change. Annual profit is £100,000. There is little likelihood that this will provoke new competition this year.

Option 2: Raise prices by 50%. If this occurs there is a 75% chance that an entrepreneur will set up in competition this year. The Board's estimate of its annual profit in this situation would be as follows.

2A WITH a new competitor		2B WITHOUT a new competitor	
Probability	Profit	Probability	Profit
0.3	£150,000	0.7	£200,000
0.7	£120,000	0.3	£150,000

Option 3: Expand the car park quickly, at a cost of £50,000, keeping prices the same. The profits are then estimated to be like 2B above, except that the probabilities would be 0.6 and 0.4 respectively.

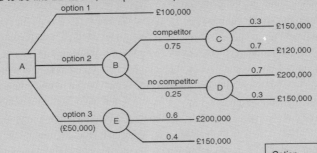

At C, expected profit = (150 × 0.3) + (120 × 0.7) = £129,000
At D, expected profit = (200 × 0.7) + (150 × 0.3) = £185,000
At B, expected profit = (129 × 0.75) + (185 × 0.25) = £143,000
At E, expected profit = (200 × 0.6) + (150 × 0.4) = £180,000

Option	Expected profit £'000
1	100
2	143
3 (180 – 50)	130

The value of perfect information

1. Work out the EVs of all options and see which is best.

2. See what decision would be taken with perfect information (if all the outcomes were known in advance with certainty) and calculate the EV.

3. The value of the information (the amount one should be willing to pay to obtain it)
   = EV of the action you would take *with* the information – EV without the information.

Alternatively a decision tree can be used.

Example

	Profit if strong demand	Profit/(loss) if weak demand
Option A	£4,000	£(1,000)
Option B	£1,500	£600
Probability	0.3	0.7

EV of A = $4,000 \times 0.3 + (1,000) \times 0.7$ = £500
EV of B = $1,500 \times 0.3 + 600 \times 0.7$ = £870
∴ Choose B

With perfect information, if demand is strong choose A but if demand is weak choose B.

∴ EV with perfect information = $0.3 \times 4,000 + 0.7 \times 600$
= £1,620

∴ Value of perfect information = £(1,620 – 870)
= £750

The value of imperfect information

The calculation of the value of imperfect information requires the use of **posterior probabilities**. These can be established by drawing a decision tree or using Bayes' theorem, but the safest way is to use tabulation (see the example which follows).

If you do decide to use Bayes' theorem, you need to remember:

$$P(B/A) = \frac{P(A \text{ and } B)}{P(A)} = \frac{P(B)P(A/B)}{P(A)}$$

Once calculated, the probabilities can be inserted on the branches of a decision tree and EVs calculated using rollback analysis.

> If the examiner asks you to calculate the maximum amount that should be paid for a forecast you need to calculate the value of imperfect information!

> This topic is ideally suited to being examined in the OT section of the exam.

Example

X Ltd is trying to decide whether or not to build a shopping centre. The probability that the centre will be successful based on past experience is 0.6.

X Ltd could conduct market research to help with the decision.

- If the centre is going to be successful there is a 75% chance that the market research will say so.
- If the centre is not going to be successful there is a 95% chance that the survey will say so.

The information can be tabulated as follows.

		Actual			
		Success	Failure	Total	
Research	Success	** 45	2	47	* given
	Failure	*** 15	38	53	** 0.75 × 60
Total		* 60	40	100	*** balancing figure

The probabilities are as follows.

| P (research says success) | = 0.47 |
| P (research says failure) | = 0.53 |

If the survey says success

| P (success) | = 45/47 | = 0.957 |
| P (failure) | = 2/47 | = 0.043 |

If the survey says failure

| P (success) | = 15/53 | = 0.283 |
| P (failure) | = 38/53 | = 0.717 |

The value of imperfect information = difference between (EV if open shopping centre without performing market research) and (EV if conduct market research and then decide whether or not to open the shopping centre).

Monte Carlo method

1 Identify the probabilities of particular variable values occurring.

2 Allocate a range of numbers to each possible variable value in proportion to the probabilities.

- Probability to 1 decimal place ➤ 10 numbers (0-9), probability to 2 decimal places ➤ 100 numbers (00-99) and so on

- A probability of 0.15 gets 0.15 of the total numbers to be assigned, that is 15 numbers: (00, 01, 02, 03, ..., 14)

3 Run the simulation model so that random numbers are generated (either manually or by a computer).

4 Allocate variable values on the basis of the generated random numbers.

Example

Daily demand Units	Probability	Numbers assigned
17	0.15	00-14
18	0.45	15-59
19	0.40	60-99
	1.00	

Random numbers for a simulation over three days are 761301.

Day	Random number	Demand
1	76	19
2	13	17
3	01	17

13: Forecasting and managing future costs

Topic List

Learning curve

Life cycle costing

Target costing

Value analysis

Most of the topics covered in this chapter and the next two are relatively 'new' and may appear to solve a lot of the problems faced by management today. It is up to you to decide whether you think they are radical new ideas or just a case of old techniques revamped and renamed!

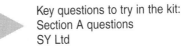

Key questions to try in the kit:
Section A questions
SY Ltd

Theory

As **cumulative output doubles**, the **cumulative average time per unit** produced **falls** to a fixed percentage of the previous cumulative average time per unit.

> Note that cumulative average time = average time per unit for all units produce so far, back to and including the first unit made.

When does learning curve theory apply?

- Product made largely by labour effort
- Brand new or relativity short-lived product
- Complex product made in small quantities for special orders

Example

Assume a 90% learning effect applies.

Cumulative output Units		Cumulative average time per unit Hours		Total time required Hours	Incremental time taken Total hours		Hours/unit
1		50.00	(× 1)	50.0			
2*	(× 90%)	45.00	(× 2)	90.0	40.0	(÷ 1)	40.0
4*	(× 90%)	40.50	(× 4)	162.0	72.0	(÷ 2)	36.0
8*	(× 90%)	36.45	(× 8)	291.6	129.6	(÷ 4)	32.4

* Output doubled each time

Formula for the learning curve

The learning effect can be shown as a learning curve.

> The formula for learning curve (a) shown above is
>
> $Y_x = aX^b$
>
> where Y = cumulative average time per unit
>
>   X = the number of units made so far
>
>   a = the time for the first unit
>
>   b = the learning coefficient or index
>
>   = log of learning rate / log of 2

This formula will be provided in the exam if it is needed.

> To derive the learning rate you need to use the learning curve formula 'in reverse'

Costs affected by the learning curve effect

- As the learning effect is a function of labour, only labour costs and other variable costs directly dependent on labour are affected.

- Materials should not be affected unless early on in the learning process they are used inefficiently.

- Fixed overhead expenditure should be unaffected (but some problems might be caused in an organisation that uses absorption costing).

Learning curve	Life cycle costing	Target costing	Value analysis

Where the learning effect might impact

- Sales projections, advertising expenditure and delivery date commitments
- Recruitment of new labour
- Calculation of productivity bonus
- Work scheduling and overtime decisions
- Budgeting with standard costs
- Cash flow projections (reducing unit variable costs)
- Market share

Where learning curve theory can be used

- To calculate the marginal (incremental) cost of making extra units of a product
- To quote selling prices for a contract, where prices are calculated at a cost plus a percentage mark-up for profit
- To prepare realistic production budgets and more efficient production schedules
- To prepare realistic standard costs for cost control purposes

Cost experience curves

The term applied to the 'corporate embodiment' of the shop floor, managerial and technological learning effects within an organisation.

It expresses the way in which the average cost per unit of production changes over time due to technological and organisational changes, not just 'learning' by skilled workers.

- Material costs will decrease slightly due to quantity discounts.
- Variable overheads will follow the pattern of direct labour.
- As volumes increase, fixed overhead per unit falls.

It is best exploited by growth and achieving a sizeable market share, so that an organisation can benefit from mass production techniques.

Limitations of learning curve theory

- Learning curve effect is not always present.
- It assumes stable conditions which allow learning to take place.
- It assumes a certain degree of motivation amongst employees.
- Breaks between repeating production of an item must not be too long or workers will forget and learning will have to begin again.
- It may be difficult to obtain enough accurate data to decide what the learning factor is.
- Learning will eventually cease.

The product life cycle

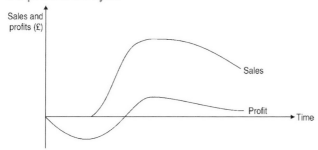

Sales and profits (£)

Sales

Profit

Time

Stages in the life cycle

- Introduction
- Growth
- Maturity
- Decline

The stage a product is at in its life cycle will affect the returns expected.

Performance measures	Introduction	Growth	Maturity	Decline
Cash	Net user	Net user	Generator	Generator
Return on capital	Not important	Not important	Important	Important
Growth	Vital	Vital	Grow with new uses	Negative growth
Profit	Not expected	Important	Important	Very important

Life cycle costing

The profiling of cost over a product's life, including the pre-production stage

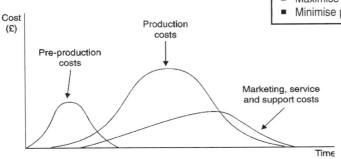

Impact on marketing strategies

As a product progresses through its life cycle, it faces different challenges and opportunities which require changes in the marketing mix and alternative marketing strategies.

Example: During the maturity stage, incentives should be given to entice competitors' customers to switch.

13: Forecasting and managing future costs

Traditional management accounting systems

- Such systems are based on the financial year and so dissect the product life cycle into a series of annual sections. Profitability is thus assessed on an annual basis.

- Such systems total all non-production costs and record them as a period expense.

- They write off R&D expenditure against revenue from existing products so that existing products seem less profitable and are scrapped too quickly.

Customer life cycle

- Aim is to extend the life cycle of a particular customer.

- Do this by encouraging loyalty (eg loyalty cards).

- Customers become more profitable over their life cycle (eg bank customers)

v Life cycle costing

- This approach tracks and accumulates a product's actual costs and revenues over the entire product life cycle, which means that a product's total profitability can be determined.

- It traces non-production costs to individual products over complete life cycles.

Benefits of life cycle costing

- Full understanding of individual product profitability

- More accurate feedback information

- Cost reduction/minimisation and revenue expansion opportunities more apparent

- Increased visibility of non-production costs

Traditional approach to product costing

1 Develop a product

2 Determine the expected standard production cost

3 Set a selling price (probably based on cost)

4 Resulting profit

Costs are controlled through variance analysis at monthly intervals.

versus

Target costing approach

Competitive market price — Set according to what the competition is charging or, if the product is new, set using market research or **functional analysis/pricing by function**

− Desired profit margin — As determined by the organisation's strategic profit plans

= **Target cost** — Resulting cost that must be achieved

Target cost

When a product is first manufactured, the target cost may be well below currently achievable cost but management will set benchmarks for improvement towards the target cost by specified dates and will incorporate them into the budgeting process.

Even if the product can be produced to target cost, once it goes into production the target cost will gradually be reduced. The reductions will be incorporated into the budgeting process, which means that cost savings must be actively sought. **Value analysis** can be used to reduce costs if and when targets are missed.

Options available to reduce cost

- Develop the product in an atmosphere of continuous improvement.
- Apply value engineering techniques.
- Collaborate closely with suppliers.
- Change production methods.
- Improve technologies/processes.
- Cut out non-value added activities.

Cost tables

These useful value engineering tools are high-volume, computerised databases of detailed cost information based on various manufacturing variables. They are a source of information about the effect on product costs of using different resources, designs and so on.

Target costing versus standard costing

	Standard costing	**Target costing**
How costs are controlled	Costs must be kept within predetermined standard costs. Variances are calculated to check that this has happened.	There is no cost slashing but continual pressure to ensure costs are kept to a minimum.
Relationship between product concept, cost and price	Predetermined product design ⬇ Cost ⬇ Price	Product design concept ⬇ Selling price ⬇ Target cost ⬆ Profit margin
Link with strategic plans	None. The approach is short-term cost control through variance analysis.	The product concept and target profit margin take into account medium-term strategic plans.
Time frame for cost control	Standards are usually revised annually.	Continual cost reduction. Target costs are revised monthly.

Value analysis (VA) is a planned, scientific approach to cost reduction which reviews the material composition of a product and the production design so that modifications and improvements can be made which do not reduce the value of the product to the customer/user.

Benefits
- Lower costs
- Better products
- Higher profits

are achieved by
- cost elimination/prevention
- cost reduction
- improving product quality and so selling more at the same price
- improving product quality and so increasing selling price

Aspects of a product's value to consider

- **Cost** value – cost of producing/selling it
- **Exchange** value – its market value
- **Use** value – what it does
- **Esteem** value – prestige customer attaches to it

Conventional cost reduction techniques v **Value analysis**

Try to achieve the lowest production cost for a specific product design

Tries to find the least cost method of making a product that achieves its desired function

Typical considerations in VA

- Can a cheaper (but as good or better) substitute material be found?
- Can unnecessary weight or embellishments be removed without reducing the product's attractiveness or desirability?
- Is it possible to use standardised or fewer components?

Functional analysis

This is most commonly applied during the development stage of products and uses the functions of a product/service (such as 'to make a mark' for a pen) as the basis for cost management.

Value engineering

The application of similar techniques to those of VA to new products, with the aim of designing and developing new products of a given value at minimum cost

Steps in a VA study

1. Select a product/service for investigation.
2. Obtain and record information about it.
3. Analyse this information and evaluate the product, considering each aspect of value in turn.
4. Consider alternatives.
5. Select the least-cost alternative for recommending to management.
6. Make a recommendation.
7. If accepted, implement the recommendation.
8. After a period, evaluate the outcome and measure the cost savings.

Topic List

Activity based costing (ABC)

Activity based management (ABM)

Business process re-engineering (BPR)

This chapter continues the theme of cost management introduced in Chapter 13.

Key questions to try in the kit:
Section A questions
LM Hospital

Cost analysis in the modern business environment

Short-term variable costs that vary with production volume

Long-term variable costs (often costs of support activities) that vary according to the range and complexity of production

Volume versus variety

The problem of producing a small number of products in volume compared with producing a large variety of products in small runs

The modern philosophy of manufacturing in variety leads to an increase in the costs of support services.

Cost control requires that costs of support activities are related to products via their casual factors.

The ABC approach is to relate the cost of support activities to cost drivers.

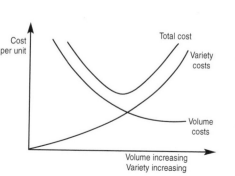

Cost drivers

Any factor which causes a change in the cost of an activity

For long-term variable costs

These are related to the transactions/activities undertaken in support departments where the costs are incurred.

∴ Cost driver = transaction/activity in support department

For short-term variable costs

Cost driver = volume of activity (eg labour hrs)

ABC and decision making

Many supporters of ABC claim it can assist with strategic decisions such as:

- Pricing strategy

- Make or buy decisions

- Promoting or discontinuing products or parts of the business

- Developing and designing products

Types of transaction

- Logistical – organise flow of resources

- Balancing – ensure demand and supply of resources are matched

- Quality – ensure production is at the required quality level

- Change – ensure customers' requirements are met

The ABC process

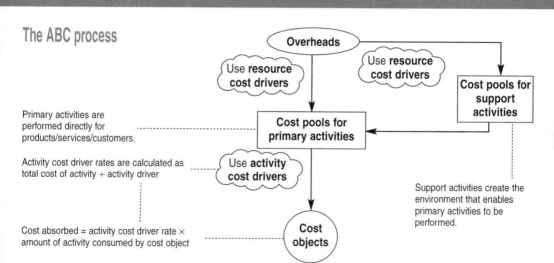

Primary activities are performed directly for products/services/customers.

Activity cost driver rates are calculated as total cost of activity ÷ activity driver

Cost absorbed = activity cost driver rate × amount of activity consumed by cost object

Support activities create the environment that enables primary activities to be performed.

Merits of ABC	Criticisms of ABC
■ Absorption costing tends to allocate too great a proportion of overheads to high-volume products (which cause relatively little diversity) and too small a proportion to low-volume products (which cause greater diversity and use more support services), whereas ABC traces a more appropriate amount. This has implications for pricing.	■ More complex than absorption costing and so should only be introduced if it will provide additional management information
	■ Tends to burden low-volume (new) products with a punitive level of overhead and so could threaten innovation
■ Ideally suited to CPA and can be used in service organisations	■ Can one cost driver explain the behaviour of all the items in a cost pool?
■ Help with cost reduction	■ Some measure of arbitrary cost apportionment needed for costs such as rent and rates
■ Takes product costing beyond traditional factory floor boundaries and considers overhead functions, such as product design and quality control	■ Do decisions or the passage of time cause costs rather than activities? Or is there no clear cause of cost?

Aspects of ABM

- **Cost reduction** (controlling/reducing the incidence of cost drivers)

- **Activity analysis**
  - Value-added and non-value-added ■
  - Core/primary, support and diversionary/discretionary

- **Design decisions** (providing cost driver information to ensure production of low cost products meeting customers' requirements)

- **Cost driver analysis**

- **Continuous improvement** (eliminating non-value-added activities)

- **Performance evaluation** (using measures relating to volume, time, quality and cost driver rates)

- **Benchmarking** (internal, functional, competitive and strategic)

Manufacturing cost hierarchy of activities

Classification	Cause	Type of cost
Unit level	Production/delivery of a single unit	Direct materials
Batch level	Group of things being made/processed/handled	Set-ups
Product/process level	Development/production/ acquisition of different items	Product development
Organisational/ facility level	Maintenance of buildings and facilities	Organisational advertising

Processing time is made up of:

- Production/performance time
- Inspection time
- Transfer time
- Idle time

Only production time is value added.

Sometimes non-value-added activities arise because of inadequacies in existing processes and so they cannot be eliminated unless these inadequacies are addressed.

Business process re-engineering

The **fundamental** rethinking and **radical** redesign of business **processes** to achieve **dramatic** improvements in critical contemporary measures of performance such as cost, quality, service and speed.

A process is a collection of activities that takes one or more kinds of input and creates an output.

Principles of BPR which influence systems development

- Processes should achieve a desired outcome (not focus on existing tasks).
- Personnel who use output from a process should perform the process.
- There is no differentiation between information gathering and information processing.
- Geographically-dispersed resources should be treated as if they were centralised.
- Parallel activities should be linked, not integrated.
- There is no distinction between workers and managers.
- Information should be captured once, at source.

15: Contemporary techniques

Topic List

Changing business environment

JIT and backflush costing

TOC and TA

Kaisen costing and CI

TQM

You need to be able to evaluate the actual and potential impacts of the techniques covered in this chapter on inventory, costs and organisational efficiency.

Key questions to try in the kit:
Section A questions
Standard costing, TQM and JIT
Cost management techniques again
MN Ltd

Changing competitive environment

	Then	Now
Manufacturing organisations	Pre 1970s, there was little overseas competition, costs were passed on to customers, minimal efforts were made to maximise efficiency/reduce costs/improve management practices.	There is massive overseas competition, and global networks for acquiring raw materials and distributing high quality, low-priced goods.
Service organisations	Pre 1980s, many were government-owned monopolies or protected by highly regulated, non-competitive environments. Cost increases were covered by increasing prices. Cost systems were not deemed necessary.	Privatisation and deregulation has resulted in intense competition, an increasing product range and a need for sophisticated costing systems.
Product life cycles	Organisations could rely on years of high demand for products.	Competitive environment, technological innovation and discriminating and sophisticated customer demand require continual product redesign and quick time to market.

Changing customer requirements

Successful organisations make customer satisfaction their priority.

Key success factors

- Cost efficiency
- Quality
- Time
- Innovation

New management approaches

- Continuous improvement
- Employee empowerment
- Total value chain analysis

Changing manufacturing systems

Traditional manufacturing systems

- Jobbing industries
- Batch processing
- Mass/flow production

Recent developments

- Group technology/repetitive manufacturing
- Dedicated cell layout

> Manufacturing processes must be sufficiently flexible both to accommodate new product design and to satisfy the demand for greater product diversity.

To compete, organisations need to......

- Be innovative and flexible
- Be able to deal with short product life cycles
- Be able to offer product variety whilst maintaining or reducing costs
- Reduce set-up times and inventories
- Have the greatest possible manufacturing flexibility

AMT helps them to do this.

- Computer-aided design (CAD)
- Computer-aided manufacturing (CAM)
- Flexible manufacturing systems (FMS)
- Electronic data interchange (EDI)

Production management strategies

The **traditional approach** to determining materials requirements is to monitor the level of stocks constantly so that once they fall to a preset level they can be re-ordered. This ignores relationships between different stock lines (demand for a particular item is dependent on demand for assemblies/subassemblies of which it forms a part).

Modern computer techniques integrate such relationships into the stock ordering process.

Production management strategies linked to AMT

- Materials requirement planning (MRPI)
- Manufacturing resource planning (MRPII)
- Enterprise resource planning (ERP)
- Optimised production technology (OPT)
- Just-in-time (JIT)

JIT systems

Traditional responses to the problems of improving manufacturing capacity and reducing unit costs of production

- Longer production runs
- Economic batch quantities
- Fewer products in the product range
- More overtime
- Reduced time on preventative maintenance, to keep production flowing

Just-in-time systems challenge such 'traditional' views.

Although often described as a technique, JIT is more of a philosophy since it encompasses a commitment to continuous improvement and a search for excellence in the design and operation of the production management system.

Aims of JIT

- Minimise warehousing and storage costs.

- Eliminate waste by maintaining control over quality of stocks input to the production process.

- Reduce the amount of raw materials and WIP carried as working capital through more effective production planning.

- Reduce the amount of finished goods held as working capital.

15: Contemporary techniques

Elimination of waste, involvement of all staff and continuous improvement are the three key elements of the JIT philosophy.

JIT techniques and methodologies

- Work standards
- Flexibility in responsibilities
- Equality of all staff
- Autonomy
- Development of personnel
- Quality of working life
- Creativity
- Design for manufacture

- Use several, small, simple machines
- Work floor layout and work flow
- Total productive maintenance
- Set-up reductions
- Total people involvement
- Visibility
- JIT purchasing

A **kanban** control system controls the flow of materials between one stage of a process and the next.

Problems with JIT

- Can be difficult to predict patterns of demand
- Makes the organisation vulnerable to disruptions in the supply chain
- Wide geographical spread makes its operation difficult

| In a JIT environment, stock levels should be low. | | Bulk of manufacturing costs should be cost of sales (not stock). | | Stock valuation is less relevant. | | Stock valuation can be simplified. |

Backflush costing

A simplified standard costing system for allocating total costs between stocks and cost of goods sold, which attempts to eliminate the need to make detailed accounting transactions (a non-value-added activity)

Accounting entries

- One or two **trigger points** determine when entries are made in the accounting system.
  - When materials are purchased/received (but not in a true JIT system where no stocks are held)
  - When goods are completed/sold
- Actual conversion costs are recorded as incurred.
- Conversion costs are applied to products at the second trigger point based on standard cost.
- Any conversion costs not applied to products are c/f and disposed of at the period end.
- The WIP account is eliminated.

> The successful operation of backflush costing rests upon predictable levels of efficiency and stable material prices and usage (ie no significant cost variances).

Problems with backflush costing

- ☒ It is only acceptable for external financial reporting if stocks are low or practically unchanged from one period to the next.
- ☒ Production controls are needed to ensure cost control during the production process.
- ☒ It is only appropriate if production and sales are approximately equal.

Advantages of backflush costing

- ☑ It is simple.
- ☑ The number of accounting entries is greatly reduced.
- ☑ It should discourage managers from producing simply for stock.

Example: two trigger points

				£	£
Purchase of raw materials	£16,000				
Conversion costs incurred	£12,700	DR	Raw materials control	16,000	
Sales and production	5,000 units	CR	Creditors		16,000
No opening stock of raw materials, WIP or		DR	Conversion costs control	12,700	
finished goods		CR	Creditors		12,700
	£	DR	Finished goods stock (5,000 × £5.80)	29,000	
Standard cost per unit		CR	Raw materials control (5,000 × £3.20)		16,000
Raw materials	3.20	CR	Conversion costs allocated (5,000 × £2.60)		13,000
Conversion costs	2.60	DR	Cost of goods sold (5,000 × £5.80)	29,000	
	5.80	CR	Finished goods stock		29,000
		DR	Conversion costs allocated	13,000	
		CR	Cost of goods sold		300
		CR	Conversion costs control		12,700

Theory of constraints (TOC)

> An **approach to production management** which aims to maximise sales revenue less material and variable overhead costs. It focuses on the factors which act as constraints to this maximisation.

Binding constraint

> A process that acts as a bottleneck (or limiting factor) and constrains throughput

Principles

Stock costs money in terms of storage space and interest and so is undesirable.

- The only stock that should be held is a buffer stock immediately prior to the bottleneck so that output through it is never held up.
- Operations prior to the binding constraint should operate at the same speed as the binding constraint otherwise WIP will build up.

Aim

Maximise **throughput contribution** (sales revenue less material cost) while keeping **conversion cost** (all operating costs accept material cost) and **investment cost** (stock, equipment, building costs etc) to a minimum.

> **TOC is not an accounting system. It is a production system.**

Throughput accounting (TA)

An **approach to accounting,** in line with the JIT philosophy, which assumes management have a given set of resources available (existing buildings, capital equipment, labour force). Using these resources, purchased materials and parts must be processed to generate sales revenue. The most appropriate financial objective to set is therefore maximisation of throughput (sales revenue less direct material cost).

Why is TA different?

TA differs from other accounting systems because of what it **emphasises.**

1st **Throughput**

2nd **Stock minimisation**

Cost control

Examples

Throughput accounting can be used successfully in service and retail industries.

- If there is a delay in processing a potential customer's application, business can be lost.
- A bottleneck might form if work that could be done by nurses has to be carried out by doctors.

Three concepts upon which TA is based

1. All factory costs except materials costs are fixed.

2. The ideal inventory level is zero (apart from a buffer stock prior to the bottleneck) and so unavoidable idle capacity is inevitable.

3. No value is added and no profit is made until a sale takes place.

Factors that limit throughput

- Bottleneck resources
- Lack of product quality/reliability
- Unreliable material supplies
- Customers with particular demands

Throughput measures

- **Return per time period***

  Throughput contribution ÷ time period

- **Return per time period on bottleneck resource***

  Throughput contribution ÷ minutes (say) on bottleneck resource

- **TA ratio***

  Throughput contribution per time period ÷ conversion cost (ie labour + o/head) per time period

- **Current effectiveness ratio**

  Standard minutes of throughput achieved ÷ minutes available

* Based on **throughput contribution** or **return** or **value added** = sales − material costs

Criticisms of TA	Advantages of TA
■ It is seen by some as too short term, as all costs other than direct material cost are regarded as fixed. ■ It concentrates on direct material cost and does not control other costs. ■ By attempting to maximise throughput an organisation could be producing in excess of profit-maximising output.	The principal advantage of TA is that it directs attention to critical factors. ■ Bottlenecks ■ Key elements in making profit ■ Inventory reduction ■ Reducing response time to customer demand ■ Even production flow ■ Overall effectiveness and efficiency

Kaizen costing

Focuses on obtaining small incremental cost reductions during the production stage of the product life cycle using various tools such as value analysis and functional analysis

Kaizen costing process

Standard costing v Kaizen costing

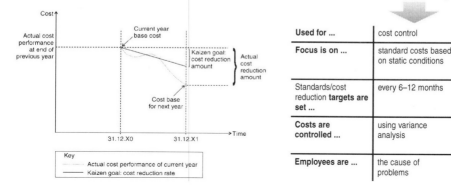

Used for ...	cost control	cost reduction
Focus is on ...	standard costs based on static conditions	actual costs assuming dynamic conditions
Standards/cost reduction **targets are set** ...	every 6–12 months	monthly
Costs are controlled ...	using variance analysis	by implementing continuous improvement
Employees are ...	the cause of problems	the source of solutions

Continuous improvement (CI)

The use of an organisation's human resources to produce a constant stream of improvements in all aspects of customer value, including quality, functional design and timely delivery, while lowering cost at the same time

Essential factors for CI

- Commitment from senior management
- Opportunity for all employees to contribute
- Information about the organisation's environment
- Employees' awareness of their role
- Management of the performance and contribution of employees
- Good communications
- Recognised quality management systems and standards
- Measurement and evaluation of progress against key performance indicators and benchmarks

Basic concepts of CI

- Quality (defined by the needs of both internal and external customers)
- Process improvements (through technology and innovative ideas)
- Team work (in the form of quality circles and group problem–solving activities)

15: Contemporary techniques

Total Quality Management (TQM)

The process of focusing on quality in the management of *all* resources and relationships within the organisation

Two basic principles of TQM

Getting things right first time, on the basis that the cost of correcting mistakes is greater than the cost of preventing them from happening in the first place

Continuous improvement – the belief that it is always possible to improve, no matter how high quality may be already

Measuring and controlling quality

1   **Quality assurance** (supplier guarantees quality)

2   **Inspection of output** (at various key stages)

3   **Monitoring customer reaction**

Employees and quality

- Workers are **empowered** and encouraged to become **multiskilled.**
- Workers are encouraged to **take responsibility** for their work.

Internal customers and suppliers

To satisfy external customers' expectations, the expectations of internal customers at each stage of the overall operation must be satisfied. Internal customers are therefore linked in quality chains.

Cost of quality

The difference between the actual cost of producing, selling and supporting products/ services and the equivalent cost if there were no failures during production/usage

Cost of prevention
Costs incurred prior to or during production in order to prevent substandard or defective products/services from being produced

Cost of appraisal
Costs incurred in order to ensure that outputs produced meet required quality standards

Cost of internal failure
Costs arising from inadequate quality which are identified before the transfer of ownership from supplier to purchaser

Cost of external failure
Costs arising from inadequate quality discovered after the transfer of ownership from supplier to purchaser

Examples

Cost of prevention
Training in quality control

Cost of appraisal
Inspection of goods inwards

Cost of internal failure
Losses due to lower selling prices for sub-quality goods

Cost of external failure
Cost of customer service section

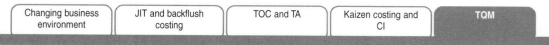
Traditional view of quality costs

The **costs of conformance** (cost of achieving specified quality standards) is a discretionary cost incurred with the intention of eliminating non-conformance costs (cost of failure to deliver the required standard of quality). The cost of non-conformance can only be reduced by increasing the cost of conformance. The optimal investment in conformance costs is when total costs of quality reach a minimum (which may be below 100% quality conformance).

Alternative view of quality costs

It is inappropriate to think of an optimal level of quality at which some failures will occur, and the inevitability of errors is not something that an organisation should accept. It is better to spend more on prevention as this will eventually lead to lower total quality costs, because appraisal, internal and external failure costs will be reduced. The emphasis should be on 'getting things right first time' and designing in quality to the product or service.

Cost of quality reports

- Such reports show how much is being spent on each of the categories.
- They indicate how total cost can be reduced by more sensible division of costs between the categories.
- Non-financial measures (eg number of warranty claims) may be more appropriate for lower-level managers.

16: Externally–orientated techniques

This chapter covers externally-orientated management accounting techniques and how they can be used to secure competitive advantage.

Topic List

Value chain

Supply chain management

Outsourcing and gain sharing

Customer profitability analysis (CPA)

Activity-based profitability analysis

Pareto analysis

Direct product profitability (DPP)

Key questions to try in the kit:
Section A questions
S&P Products plc
FF plc

The value chain is a model of the nine organisational activities (which procure outputs, process them and add value to them in some way, to generate outputs for customers) and the relationships between them.

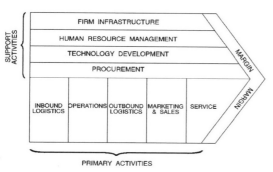

PRIMARY ACTIVITIES

Focus of the value chain

The focus is external, not only in relation to competitors but also back to suppliers and forward to customers. Traditional management accounting, in contrast, has an internal focus.

The value chain and competitive advantage

Competitive advantage is gained either from providing better customer value for equivalent cost or equivalent customer value for lower cost. Value chain analysis is therefore essential to determine where in an organisation's value chain costs can be lowered or value enhanced.

The traditional view is that to improve profitability it is necessary to get the lowest price from suppliers and to obtain the best price from customers next in line down the supply chain. **Supply chain management** looks at the supply chain as a whole, and starts with the view that all organisations in the supply chain collaborate to produce something of value for the end customer.

Advantages

- By adding value within the supply chain, customer satisfaction will be improved and customers will pay more.
- Organisations can benefit by reducing waste and inefficiency at the interface between organisations within the supply chain.

Issues facing supply chain managers

- Production
- Supply
- Inventory
- Location
- Transportation
- Information

Managing the supply chain calls for understanding and knowledge of:

- Customer demand patterns
- Service level requirements
- Distance considerations
- Cost

Using technology

EDI, the Internet and software applications have had a huge impact on supply chain management as suppliers know what a customer needs before the customer asks.

16: Externally–orientated techniques

Choosing activities to outsource

An activity is a candidate for outsourcing unless the organisation must control it to maintain its competitive position or if the organisation can deliver to a level comparable with the best organisations in the world.

Current trends in outsourcing

In an effort to cut costs, many organisations are now outsourcing activities both nearshore (such as Eastern Europe) and offshore (such as the Far East and India).

Partnering

To minimise the risks associated with outsourcing, organisations generally enter into long-run contracts with suppliers that specify costs, quality and delivery. They build close partnerships or alliances with a few key suppliers, collaborating on design and manufacturing decisions and building a culture and commitment for quality and timely delivery.

Incentivisation

Incentives should encourage suppliers to provide benefits significantly beyond those contracted for.

Gain-sharing arrangements

All cost overruns and cost savings are shared between the customer and contractor.

Customer profitability analysis (CPA)

The analysis of the revenues and costs associated with specific customers or customer groups

The relative profitability of specific customers/customer groups can be assessed, and strategies aimed at attracting and retaining the most profitable customers implemented.

Customers can be categorised using this grid.

- The aim is to attract as many accepting customers as possible.

- Many large retail organisations fall into the demanding category.

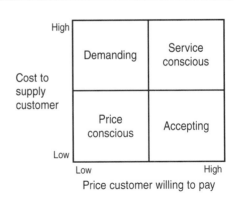

CPA and ABC

The necessary analysis of costs can be successfully carried out using ABC cost drivers.

Examples

Cost	Cost driver
Delivery	Miles travelled
After sales service and support	Number of visits

Unprofitable customers identified by CPA should be persuaded to alter their buying behaviour (eg discouraged from placing lots of small orders).

The ABC approach also highlights where cost reduction efforts should be focused (eg reduce ordering cost).

Customer profitability statement

Example

	£'000	£'000
Revenue at list prices		X
Less: discounts given		X
Net revenue		X
Less: cost of goods sold		X
Gross margin		X
Less: customer specific costs		X
Less: financing costs		
credit period	X	
customer specific inventory	X	
		X
Net margin from customer		X

Customer life cycles

Customers can be costed over their life cycle and expected future cash flows discounted.

By applying the concept of the manufacturing cost hierarchy (Chapter 14), the costs of products, customers and distribution channels can be compared with their revenues and a tier of contribution levels established.

Unit-level product contributions

Product contributions after deducting batch-related expenses

Product contributions after deducting product-sustaining expenses

Product-line contributions after deducting product-line sustaining expenses

Plant profit after deducting facility-sustaining expenses

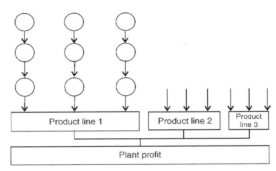

Costs should be assigned to the appropriate level in the hierarchy (depending on whether they are incurred in relation to an activity that supports a product/product line/customer/distribution channel). Costs should then be aggregated down the hierarchy to determine contribution margins by product/product line/customer/distribution channel.

Pareto analysis

This basically means finding out what proportion of a total is represented by each of the individual things making up the total. For example, here is a Pareto analysis of sales.

Example (for sales)

Product	Sales Units	Sales %	Cumulative sales Units	Cumulative sales %
A	1,000	43	1,000	43
B	800	35	1,800	78
C	500	22	2,300	100
	2,300	100		

A similar analysis could be done for any other aspect of product data: contribution, cost, complaints or whatever.

Using Pareto analysis

You might have to do a Pareto analysis of sales levels as compared with contribution or amount of stock held.

Typically this reveals that the products/ divisions that sell the most are different from the products/divisions that provide the highest contribution or have the highest levels of stocks.

This may suggest management action such as the revision of pricing policy or the discontinuance of certain products.

80/20 rule

Strictly speaking 'Pareto' is synonymous with the 80/20 rule - 80% of something is accounted for by 20% of something else (for example 80% of stock value is represented by only 20% of stock items).

This should not be interpreted too literally - the basic principle is that a few items or activities are often core to an organisation's fortunes while the majority are only peripheral.

Example

If an organisation uses ABC, a pareto analysis of cost drivers might show that, say, 15% of cost drivers are responsible for 80% of total cost.

Diagrammatic representation

Various forms are possible.

Pareto curve of sales

CPA and Pareto's rule

Pareto's rule is often found to apply (20% of customers generate approximately 80% of total margin).

16: Externally–orientated techniques

DPP

A costing system used primarily within the retail sector. It involves the attribution of costs other than purchase price (eg warehousing) to each product line. A net profit, as opposed to a gross profit, can therefore be identified for each product.

Why is DPP important?

- Gross profit includes none of the organisation's own costs and so provides little planning and control information.
- Some product categories consume more of the organisation's resources than others (eg storage) and so an attempt to relate these direct costs to products is needed.

Direct product costs and profit

Direct product profit is the contribution a product category makes to fixed costs and profits.

> Sales price
> − Purchase price
> _____
> Gross margin
> + Other direct revenues
> − Direct product costs
> _____
> Direct product profit
> _____

Only occur occasionally (eg if the retailer receives a discount from the manufacturer for point of sale promotion)

Direct product costs can be directly attributed to the handling and storing of individual products.

Examples

- Warehouse direct costs (eg space costs)
- Transport direct costs (eg fuel)
- Store/supermarket direct costs (eg shelf filling)

Confusingly, direct product costs also contain some level of indirect cost, apportioned on the basis of product characteristics (eg cost of shelf space apportioned by means of physical volume).